Other Bantam Books in the series
Ask your bookseller for the books you have missed

AN AMERICAN CIVIL LIBERTIES UNION HANDBOOK

THE RIGHTS
OF
SINGLE PEOPLE

**Mitchell Bernard,
Ellen Levine,
Stefan Presser,
and
Marianne Stecich**

**General Editor of this series:
Norman Dorsen, President ACLU**

 120753

BANTAM BOOKS
TORONTO · NEW YORK · LONDON · SYDNEY · AUCKLAND

THE RIGHTS OF SINGLE PEOPLE
A Bantam Book / published by arrangement with
The American Civil Liberties Union
Bantam edition / April 1985

ISBN 0-553-24816-2

Published simultaneously in the United States and Canada

Bantam Books are published by Bantam Books, Inc. Its trademark, consisting of the words "Bantam Books" and the por-
trayal of a rooster, is Registered in U.S. Patent and Trademark
Office and in other countries. Marca Registrada. Bantam
Books, Inc., 666 Fifth Avenue, New York, New York 10103.

PRINTED IN THE UNITED STATES OF AMERICA

O   0 9 8 7 6 5 4 3 2 1

Acknowledgments

The authors gratefully acknowledge the assistance of the following people in the preparation of this book: Chris Hansen, Betty Kranzdorf, Marilyn Kupersmith, Carol Lefcourt, Jeffrey Miller, and Tom Stoddard.

Contents

Preface

This guide sets forth your rights under the present law, and offers suggestions on how they can be protected. It is one of a continuing series of handbooks published in cooperation with the American Civil Liberties Union (ACLU).

Surrounding these publications is the hope that Americans, informed of their rights, will be encouraged to exercise them. Through their exercise, rights are given life. If they are rarely used, they may be forgotten and violations may become routine.

This guide offers no assurances that your rights will be respected. The laws may change and, in some of the subjects covered in these pages, they change quite rapidly. An effort has been made to note those parts of the law where movement is taking place, but it is not always possible to predict accurately when the law *will* change.

Even if the laws remain the same, their interpretations by courts and administrative officials often vary. In a federal system such as ours, there is a built-in problem since state and federal law differ, not to speak of the confusion between states. In addition, there are wide variations in the ways in which particular courts and administrative officials will interpret the same law at any given moment.

If you encounter what you consider to be a specific abuse of your rights, you should seek legal assistance. There are a number of agencies that may help you, among them, ACLU affiliate offices, but bear in mind that the ACLU is a limited-purpose organization. In many communities, there are federally funded legal service offices that provide assistance to persons who cannot afford the costs of legal representation. In general, the rights that the ACLU defends are freedom of inquiry and expression, due process of law, equal protection of the laws, and privacy. The authors in this series have discussed other rights (even though they sometimes fall outside the ACLU's usual concern) in order to provide as much guidance as possible.

These books have been planned as guides for the people directly affected; therefore, the question and answer format. (In some areas there are more detailed works available for "experts.") These guides seek to raise the major issues and inform the nonspecialist of the basic law on the subject. The authors of these books are themselves specialists who understand the need for information at "street level."

If you encounter a specific legal problem in an area discussed in one of these handbooks, show the book to your attorney. Of course, he or she will not be able to rely exclusively on the handbook to provide you with adequate representation. But if your attorney hasn't had a great deal of experience in the specific area, the handbook can provide helpful suggestions on how to proceed.

Norman Dorsen, President
American Civil Liberties Union

The principal purpose of this handbook, as well as others in this series, is to inform individuals of their legal rights. The authors from time to time suggest what the law should be, but their personal views are not necessarily those of the ACLU. For the ACLU's position on the issues discussed in this handbook, the reader should write to Librarian, ACLU, 132 W. 43 Street, New York, NY 10036.

Introduction

This American Civil Liberties Union handbook concerns the rights of single people. By *single* we mean those people who have never been married or, due to death, annulment, or divorce, are no longer married. On the margin, and very much affected by the developments addressed in this book, are those people en route to dissolving an existing marriage. The discussion that follows will help to educate the reader as to the legal rights and responsibilities of single people in such areas as employment, housing, adoption, abortion, custody, personal property, finance, and the criminal law.

The rights of single people is an important topic due to the dramatic rise in the number of couples living together out of wedlock, or "cohabiting," during the last twenty-five years. Cohabitation implies an ongoing sexual relationship, whether homosexual or heterosexual, and may resemble a traditional marriage in terms of such commitments as emotional involvement. Notwithstanding similarities between cohabitation and marriage, the law may grant rights or impose obligations depending solely on the legal status of the relationship. Since it is estimated that many millions of Americans now are cohabiting, the legal distinctions become significant as well as interesting.

The large increase in the number of people cohabiting has pushed both courts and legislatures to reevaluate traditional legal doctrines. The result, in some instances, has been the creation of new rights for single people, rights that previously were reserved for married couples. In other instances, the result has been the creation of new obligations for cohabitants, particularly if the relationship dissolves. These rights and obligations cut across various classes of people as well as substantive areas of law.

Restrictions placed on the availability of abortions for

unmarried women, for example, raise traditional women's rights issues. Laws regulating sexual conduct outside the marital relationship may be enforced with particular emphasis on singles who are also homosexual. Where other ACLU handbooks deal specifically with the subgroups of singles (women and gays), we refer the reader to those texts. The focus in this book is on the issues that particularly affect single people, and particularly the ways in which laws and legal doctrines discriminate on the basis of marital status. An underlying thesis is that, where they are arbitrary—as in many instances we find them to be—these distinctions should be eliminated.

If an issue is regulated by state law (for example, whether fornication is legal), then it is imperative to check the state statute in question. Court decisions from one state do not bind courts in other jurisdictions, although they may be followed if a local court agrees with the ruling. In other words, what is prohibited in one state may be perfectly lawful across the state line. And in the case of federal law, decisions by lower courts may not be binding on the state in which a new case arises. The one exception is a decision by the United States Supreme Court which, until it is overturned, is the law of the land on all federal questions.

Partly because issues involving single people are on the cutting edge, the law in this area is changing rapidly. Consequently, litigants may be able to succeed with novel legal arguments. It also underscores the importance of checking the current law in the relevant jurisdiction and, if necessary, of contacting an attorney if a substantial legal question arises. We do not suggest that every legal problem requires a lawyer's involvement. Many people, for example, successfully draft marriage contracts on their own. However, in complex areas, such as custody or high finance, or if one is arrested for an alleged violation of a criminal statute, it is almost always advisable to contact an attorney.

I
Torts

A.
Consortium

What is "loss of consortium" and who can sue for it?

Today consortium is generally understood as a "relational interest" that a person has with respect to another family member,[1] including material factors of support and services and such nonmaterial elements as affection, emotional support, and companionship.[2] The loss of consortium is "[a]n interference with the continuance of the relation, . . . [which] may be redressed by a tort action."[3] A tort action is a civil, as opposed to criminal, proceeding to redress an injury caused by a negligent or intentional act or omission.

Originally, at common law, consortium was a husband's right. He alone could sue a negligent person (*tort feasor*) who through his or her negligence deprived the husband of sexual relations with his wife, as well as her society and her services. It was a right that arose out of the marriage relationship and was deemed a property interest of a husband in his wife.[4] Until 1950, a wife could not sue for the loss of her husband's consortium anywhere in the United States. In that year in a landmark case a court held that a wife could maintain such a suit.[5]

Today, in seven states wives are still unable to sue for the loss of consortium,[6] and in three neither spouse is able to sue.[7] Some states allow parents to sue for the loss of consortium of a child,[8] and a few permit the reciprocal suit by a child for the loss of a parent's consortium.[9]

Can unmarried cohabitants sue for the loss of consortium?

Probably not. In only three cases have courts permitted a cohabitant to sue for the loss of consortium of the other cohabitant.[10] Almost all the lawsuits, both those that allowed recovery, and those that denied it, have occurred since 1980. Thus, this is a very new claim being asserted in response to a very old but newly increasing phenomenon—cohabitation without marriage.[11]

Two of the cases allowing recovery, *Bulloch v. U.S.*, and *Sutherland v. Auch Inter-Borough Transit Co.*, were decided by federal courts interpreting, or more correctly, predicting, the direction of state law. In both instances, subsequent cases decided by the respective state courts disavowed the federal courts' holdings and found no right for a cohabitant to sue for the loss of consortium.[12]

Why can't a cohabitant sue for the loss of consortium?

The arguments generally advanced for requiring a legal marriage to bring such a suit express practical judicial concerns, legal principles, and social and moral values.[13] Practically, courts worry that if cohabitants were allowed to sue, there would be no end to the list of possible plaintiffs, such as cousins, uncles, and business colleagues.[14] In addition, there would be problems of proof concerning the significance of the relationship, whereas a marriage license represents, according to these courts, a statement of state-acknowledged significance.[15] In the same vein, it has been argued that without the formalized marriage relationship, the degree of injury and concomitant damages are pure speculation.[16] Some judges have argued that there is no legal precedent for granting the right to such a suit, and that only legislatures can make sweeping social policy changes such as, they argue, this would entail.[17]

Finally, some of the courts have been loquacious, indeed sentimental, about the importance of the institution of marriage, asserting that it is the "touchstone" of the strength of the "male-female relationship,"[18] and the "basic unit of social order."[19] One judge went so far as to suggest that if cohabitants have rights of consortium, then marriage will be denigrated, and not only children born of a marriage relationship, but also "the very fabric of society," will be bastardized.[20] Most judges merely restate the proposition that marriage is a prerequisite of a loss of consortium lawsuit.

Can persons engaged at the time of the injury and subsequently married sue for the loss of consortium?

Most courts that have addressed this issue have said no.[21] These courts have all invoked the rule that a formal marriage must exist before a consortium claim can be recognized. There is nineteenth-century precedent for this holding. In an 1890 Pennsylvania case, a court held that a husband could not sue for the loss of consortium for injuries the wife suffered before marriage.[22] In the recent cases involving engaged-then-married couples, some of the courts have stated that by marrying the injured person, the spouse seeking to sue for the loss of consortium "waived" any such right. These courts seem to be making a *caveat emptor,* or "let the buyer beware," argument for denying the claims.[23]

In only one case, *Sutherland v. Auch Inter-Borough Transit Co.,*[24] did the court allow the claim; the judge reasoned that the suit was appropriate since the couple was engaged at the time of the injury and married less than a month later. The court limited the damages to the period following the marriage.

What arguments support a consortium claim for unmarried cohabitants?

The main arguments supporting such a claim were advanced in the first major case granting the right, *Bulloch v. U.S.,*[25] and even more extensively in the most recent case, *Butcher v. Superior Court of Orange County.*[26] In both cases the couples had been together for many years, in *Bulloch* nearly thirty years (married, divorced, and reconciled), and in *Butcher* nearly twelve years (living together). In both cases, the couples had shared their financial resources and liabilities, raised children and generally lived as married couples. In light of the contemporary understanding of consortium as a "relational interest" and not a husband's property right, both courts recognized that the fundamental question was the definition of the relevant relationship. Both courts rejected the arbitrary line drawing at formal marriage. As the judge in *Butcher* said, "When it is determined that the common law or judge-made law is unjust or out of step with the times, we should have no reluctance to change it."[27] Both courts reviewed the case law following the *Marvin v. Marvin*[28] decision, the growing legal recognition of marriagelike rights of cohabitants,[29] the census data on cohabitation, and the policy arguments usually asserted for denying consortium rights to cohabitants. In *Bulloch* the court said that the policy of tort law is to compensate for injury, and that reward or punishment based on marital status is not relevant in assessing liability.[30] Tort liability is based in part on the notion of "foreseeability"; that is, the defendant owes a duty of care to persons foreseeably endangered by his actions. Thus the California Supreme Court has held that "[i]n our society the likelihood that an injured adult will be a married man or woman is substantial. . . ."[31] In light of today's changing social living arrangements, the *Butcher* court asserted, "One who negligently causes a disabling injury to an adult may also reasonably expect in our contemporary society that the injured person may be cohabiting with another without benefit of marriage."[32]

In both *Bulloch* and *Butcher*, the judges pointed out that cohabitants face the same arguments that in earlier decades had been advanced against wives trying to sue for the loss of consortium: The injury is too remote; the damages are too speculative; and there's the risk of opening the floodgates to remote plaintiffs, such as cousins, employers, coworkers, friends, etc. Both judges found that the arguments were equally unpersuasive regarding cohabitants. The court in *Butcher* said that the "suffering of an unmarried spouse may be no less real"[33] than that of a married person. In the context of a custody dispute involving an unwed father and his illegitimate children, the Supreme Court has said, "[F]amilial bonds in such cases [are] often as warm, enduring, and important as those arising within a more formally organized family unit."[34]

In sum, both courts held that to exclude all cohabitants per se is unjust, and that social change should be recognized by the courts in interpreting and carrying out the law.

If cohabitants can sue for the loss of consortium, would there be any limits on who can justifiably claim consortium rights?

Obviously not all cohabitation relationships should give rise to consortium rights. As the court in *Butcher* noted, "[O]ne-night stand[s]" are not to be included. The standard, according to the court, for evaluation is whether the relationship is both stable and significant.[35] Among the factors that can be assessed are the duration of the relationship, the degree of economic cooperation and dependence, the exclusivity of sexual relations, and a family relationship with children.[36]

NOTES

1. W. Prosser, *Handbook of the Law of Torts* 873 (4th ed. 1971).
2. *See, e.g., Millington v. Southeastern Elevator Co.*, 239 N.E. 2d 897, 899 (N.Y. 1968) ("The concept of consortium includes not only loss of support or services, it also embraces such elements as love, companionship, affection, society, sexual relations, solace and more.")
3. *Butcher v. Superior Court*, 188 Cal. Rptr. 503 (Ct. App. 1983).
4. *See, e.g., Chicago B. & Q.R. Co. v. Honey*, 63 F. 39 (8th Cir. 1894); *Mead v. Baum*, 69 A. 962, 963 (N.J. Super. 1908); Comment, Extending Consortium Rights to Unmarried Cohabitants, 129 *U. Pa. L. Rev.* 911 (1981).
5. *Hitaffer v. Argonne Co.*, 183 F.2d 811 (D.C. Cir.), *cert. denied*, 340 U.S. 852 (1950).
6. Connecticut: *Lockwood v. Wilson H. Lee Co.*, 128 A.2d 330 (Conn. 1956); Kansas: *Hoffman v. Dautel*, 388 P.2d 615 (Kan. 1964); Louisiana: *Bourque v. American Mutual Liability Insurance Co.*, 345 So. 2d 237 (La. 1977); New Mexico: *Roseberry v. Starkovich*, 387 P.2d 321 (N.M. 1963); Utah: *Ellis v. Hathaway*, 493 P.2d 985 (Utah 1972); Wyoming: *Bates v. Donnafield*, 481 P.2d 347 (Wyo. 1971). VA. CODE §55–36 (1950) abolished the husband's right to sue for the loss of consortium; in *Carey v. Foster*, 345 F.2d 772 (4th Cir. 1965), the court held that this provision also barred the loss of consortium action by wives.
7. Louisiana: *Bourque, supra* note 6; Utah: *Ellis, supra* note 6; Virginia: VA. CODE §§55–36; *Carey, supra* note 6.
8. *See, e.g., Wardlow v. City of Keokuk*, 190 N.W.2d 439 (Iowa 1971); *Shockley v. Prier*, 225 N.W.2d 495 (Wis. 1975).

9. *See, e.g., Ferriter v. Daniel O'Connell's Sons, Inc.*, 413 N.E.2d 690 (Mass. 1980); *Berger v. Weber*, 303 N.W.2d 424 (Mich. 1981). *But see Jeune v. Del E. Webb Construction Co.*, 269 P.2d 723 (Ariz. 1954) (no suit was permitted); *Borer v. American Airlines, Inc.*, 563 P.2d 858 (Cal. 1977) (no suit was permitted).

10. *Bulloch v. U.S.*, 487 F. Supp. 1078 (D.N.J. 1980) (interpreting New Jersey law); *Sutherland v. Auch Inter-Borough Transit Co.*, 366 F. Supp. 127 (E.D. Pa. 1973) [interpreting Pennsylvania law; was later disapproved by a Pennsylvania court in *Rockwell v. Liston*, 71 Pa. D. & C.2d 756 (1975)]; *Butcher, supra* note 3, the reasoning and holding were rejected by another California court of appeals in *Hendrix v. General Motors Corp.*, 193 Cal. Rptr. 922 (Cal. App. 1983).

11. In 1979, approximately 2,692,000 heterosexual couples lived in unmarried cohabitation arrangements. This figure is more than double the number in 1970. *See*, Comment, *supra* note 4, at n. 1 and the accompanying text. The incidence of cohabitation without marriage increased by 800 percent between 1960 and 1970. *See* Comment, "Consortium Rights of the Unmarried," 15 *Family L. Q.* 223, 224 (1981).

12. *Childers v. Shannon*, 444 A.2d 1141 (N.J. Super. 1981) (disavowed *Bulloch, supra* note 10); *Rockwell, supra* note 10 (disavowed *Sutherland, supra* note 10).

13. California: *Tong v. Jocson*, 142 Cal. Rptr. 726 (Ct. App. 1977); Florida: *Tremblay v. Carter*, 390 So. 2d 816 (Fla. Dist. Ct. App. 1980); Illinois: *Sostock v. Reiss*, 415 N.E.2d 1094 (Ill. App. Ct. 1980); Iowa: *Laws v. Griep*, 332 N.W.2d 339 (Iowa 1983); Kentucky: *Angelet v. Shivar*, 602 S.W.2d 185 (Ky. Ct. App. 1980); Maine: *Sawyer v. Bailey*, 413 A.2d 165 (Me. 1980); Michigan: *Chiesa v. Rowe*, 486 F. Supp. 236 (W.D. Mich. 1980); New Jersey: *Childers, supra* note 12; Pennsylvania: *Rockwell, supra* note 12.

14. *See, e.g., Butcher, supra* note 10.

15. *Id. See also Borer, supra* note 9; *Tremblay, supra* note 13; *Sawyer, supra* note 13; *Childers, supra* note 13.

16. *Id.*

17. *See, e.g., Childers, supra* note 13, 1143; ("Only a Legislature responsible to the electorate should have such power.") *Contra, Butcher, supra* note 10 (The common law must be changed when "unjust or out of step with the times.")

18. *Childers, supra* note 13, at 1142.

19. *Laws, supra* note 13, at 341.

20. *Childers, supra* note 13, at 1143.

21. *Chiesa, supra* note 13 (the injury occurred 5 months before the marriage); *Tong, supra* note 13 (the injury occurred within a month of marriage); *Tremblay, supra* note 13 (the injury delayed the marriage); *Sostock, supra* note 13 (the injury occurred less than a month before

the marriage); *Angelet, supra* note 13 (the injury occurred during the wife's childhood); *Sawyer, supra* note 13 (the injury occurred 2 months before the marriage); *Childers, supra* note 12 (the injury occurred 2 months before the marriage).

22. *Reading v. Pennsylvania Railroad,* 19 A. 321 (Pa. 1890).
23. *See, e.g., Chiesa, supra* note 13; *Sawyer, supra* note 13.
24. 366 F. Supp. 127 (E.D. Pa. 1973).
25. 487 F. Supp. 1078 (D.N.J. 1980).
26. 188 Cal. Rptr. 503 (Ct. App. 1983). *See also* Comment, *supra* note 4; Wilson, "Loss of Consortium Claims by Unmarried Cohabitants: The Roles of Private Self-Determination and Public Policy," 571 *Indiana L. J.* 605 (1982); Treu, "Loss of Consortium and Engaged Couples: The Frustrating Fate of Faithful Fiancees," 44 *Ohio St. L. J.* 219 (1983).
27. 188 Cal. Rptr. 503 (Ct. App. 1983).
28. 557 P.2d 106 (Cal. 1976).
29. *See, e.g., Bulloch, supra* note 10, at 1080.
30. *Id.* at 1084.
31. *Rodriguez v. Bethlehem Steel Corp.,* 525 P.2d 669, 680 (Cal. 1974).
32. *Butcher, supra* note 3.
33. *Id.* at 67.
34. *Stanley v. Illinois,* 405 U.S. 645, 651-52 (1972).
35. *Butcher, supra* note 3.
36. *Id.*

B.
Wrongful Death

What is a "wrongful death lawsuit" and who can sue for money damages for the wrongful death of another?

A wrongful death lawsuit is a civil action designed to compensate persons who have a legally defined close relationship with a deceased person. Every state has a wrongful death statute that defines who can sue—generally, a spouse, child, parents, or heirs, against a defendant who killed the deceased through a wrongful act, neglect, or default. The injury for which the survivor can recover is defined by statute and case law, and usually includes the loss of future support, the monetary value of services no longer performed, and in some cases the loss of companionship and comfort.

Can a cohabitant recover for the wrongful death of his or her cohabitant?

No. Currently no jurisdiction in the United States provides a wrongful death remedy for cohabitants. Some state statutes include "putative spouses" in the list of those who can bring a wrongful death action.[1] These are defined as the surviving spouses of marriages that turned out not to be legal but who believed in good faith that their marriages were valid. Courts that have dealt with the question of wrongful death claims of cohabitants have distinguished what they call meretricious spouses from putative spouses, and conclude that meretricious spouses cannot sue for the wrongful death of their cohabitants.[2] Meretricious spouses are defined as those who live together in a marriagelike situation but with the belief and knowledge that they are not in fact legally married.

What are the reasons why a cohabitant cannot recover wrongful death damages?

Since wrongful death actions are statutory, the courts that have addressed this issue find that only a legislature can include a cohabitant in the list of people who have a right to sue for wrongful death.[3] These courts have stated that legislatures could reasonably conclude that the failure to enter into a formal state-sanctioned marriage meant that couples have not shown the "permanent commitment" necessary for an award of damages.[4] These courts also reason that states have a substantial interest in promoting formal marriage, in avoiding fraudulent claims and in avoiding difficult problems of proof as to whether or not a couple had a marriagelike relationship.[5] With regard to proof questions, one court has said that putative spouses have documentary evidence—a marriage license—of participation in a marriage ceremony, while meretricious spouses would have to establish their relationship with more subjective proof.[6]

What effect have the "palimony" cases had on cohabitants' rights to wrongful death damages?

None. The landmark California case of *Marvin v. Marvin*,[7] which recognized certain contractual rights and obligations of unmarried cohabitants, has not been applied by California courts to permit unmarried cohabitants to sue for wrongful death. The courts have held that the *Marvin* case does not broaden the statutory definition of heirs to include cohabitants.[8]

With the large number of couples cohabiting today, and with no indication that the numbers are decreasing, it is likely that more cases will be brought, and a cohabitant may yet prevail. A primary argument a cohabitant is likely to make is that wrongful death statutes are intended to compensate those with intimate and enduring relationships to the decedent. Mere difficulty of proof should not bar the action. Rather, cohabitants who offer sufficient proof of an intimate and enduring relationship should be able to prevail.

Can a cohabitant sue for the wrongful death of the other cohabitant if they were planning to be married?

No. Thus far the courts have drawn a sharp line between married and nonmarried couples with respect to wrongful death claims. In a recent California case,[9] the couple was scheduled to be married eight days after the man's death; they had cohabited, pooled their expenses and earnings and jointly purchased a house. The court nonetheless held that the legislature, in not including cohabitants among those who could sue for wrongful death, could reasonably have believed (1) that the absence of a formal marriage showed the lack of necessary permanence to the relationship; (2) that the state had a strong interest in promoting marriage; and (3) that the problems of proof were too burdensome for courts to address.[10]

Can an unmarried parent recover damages for the wrongful death of her or his illegitimate child?

An unwed mother may. In *Glona v. American Guarantee & Liability Insurance Co.*,[11] the United States Supreme Court upheld a mother's challenge to a Louisiana statute that excluded all unwed mothers from the right to sue for the wrongful death of their children. According to the Court, the statute violated the equal protection clause of the Constitution by permitting married but not unmarried mothers to sue.

By contrast, a state statute can constitutionally deny an unwed father the right to sue for the wrongful death of his illegitimate child. In *Parham v. Hughes*,[12] the Supreme Court upheld a Georgia statute that denied unwed fathers who had *not* legitimated the child the right to sue for the child's wrongful death. Other Georgia statutes provided procedures for legitimating a child. The Court distinguished *Glona* by saying that in that case there was a blanket exclusion of all unwed mothers, whereas in *Parham*, the statute permitted the father to sue if he had legitimated the child. State statutes usually provide fairly uncomplicated procedures by which an unwed father can acknowledge paternity and legitimate his child. Such a procedure is not only important in the context of wrongful death actions, but is frequently significant in custody and adoption disputes.[13]

NOTES

1. *See, e.g.*, CAL. CIV. PROC. CODE §377.
2. *Vogel v. Pan American World Airways, Inc.*, 450 F. Supp. 224 (S.D.N.Y. 1978) (construing California's wrongful death statute); *Nieto v. City of Los Angeles*, 188 Cal. Rptr. 31 (Ct. App. 1982); *Garcia v. Douglas Aircraft Co.*, 184 Cal. Rptr. 390 (Ct. App. 1982).
3. *Id.* For an analysis of statutory and case law development, *see* Harris, "The Rights of Meretricious Spouses to Wrongful Death Actions, 13 *Pac. L. J.* 125 (1981).
4. *See, e.g.*, *Vogel, supra* note 2.
5. *Id.*
6. *Id.* at 226.
7. 557 P.2d 106 (Cal. 1976).
8. *Nieto, supra* note 2; *Garcia, supra* note 2.
9. *Garcia, supra* note 2.
10. *Id. See also Aspinall v. McDonnell Douglas Corp.*, 625 F.2d 325 (9th Cir. 1980) (a couple had lived together for over 4 years and the decedent left his entire estate to the woman; a wrongful death action was denied). In *Vogel, supra* note 2, the couple had been married, divorced, and after the divorce were living together.
11. 391 U.S. 73 (1968). In *Levy v. Louisiana*, 391 U.S. 68 (1968), the Supreme Court upheld the claim of 5 illegitimate children who sued for the wrongful death of their mother.
12. 441 U.S. 347 (1979).
13. For a discussion of the rights of unwed parents, *see* the ACLU Handbook, *The Rights of Parents*, by A. Sussman and M. Guggenheim (1980).

II.
Criminal Law

The criminal laws of many states discriminate against single people by prohibiting sexual activity outside the marriage relationship. This is an attempt, dating back to colonial days and before, to confine sex to marriage. Thus, many states proscribe cohabitation and fornication between unmarried persons. In addition, many states punish adultery. Moreover, sodomy laws prohibit *homosexual conduct* that, by definition, is nonmarital. And, where *sodomy* is defined to include heterosexual conduct, some states have attempted (mostly unsuccessfully) to limit the "deviant" activity to married partners. Though states do not aggressively enforce many of these laws, the effect of the prohibitions is to limit the sexual activity in which single people lawfully may engage.

There are also more subtle forms of discrimination. In the area of domestic violence there have been legislative initiatives to equalize the status of married and unmarried victims. But in at least one state this equalization has worked to the disadvantage of unmarried women by extending to cohabitants the spousal exemption from prosecution for rape and sexual abuse. And in decisions involving bail, probation, parole, and parole revocation, traditional family ties may be helpful in winning early release.

In examining the origins of, and developments in, the criminal law as it affects single people, one can see how society is struggling with laws that stem from largely outmoded sexual values.

11

What is "cohabitation"?

Cohabitation exists when two people, who are not married to one another, live together. Cohabitation includes an element of implied sexual intercourse;[1] as a result, cohabitation, for the purpose of the criminal law, means living together as part of an ongoing, nonmarital sexual liaison.

Is cohabitation against the law?

Yes, in thirteen states. The states in which cohabitation is illegal are Alabama, Arizona, Florida, Idaho, Illinois, Massachusetts, Michigan, Mississippi, New Mexico, North Dakota, South Carolina, Virginia, and West Virginia.[2] Some of these statutes have special features. In Alabama, for example, one of the cohabitants must be married in order for the cohabitation to constitute a crime.[3] Thus, in Alabama, two unmarried people may live together without violating the law. There is a modest trend against laws forbidding cohabitation. During the last several years, Alaska, Kansas, and Wisconsin have repealed anticohabitation statutes.[4]

What is the possible punishment after conviction for cohabitation?

In most of the states that outlaw cohabitation, the penalties range from 60 days to 3 years in jail, in addition to fines up to $500.[5]

Do many people cohabit notwithstanding criminal laws prohibiting it?

Yes. By 1978, 6 to 8 million Americans were cohabiting. It is estimated that the number had increased by over 700 percent during the decade 1960–70, and that from 1970–78, the number increased by 100 percent.[6] In other words, in the United States many millions of people are unmarried and living together, even in states where it is illegal.

Are laws prohibiting cohabitation frequently enforced?

No.[7] Due in part to the large number of people who cohabit, these laws are rarely enforced. Having cohabitation statutes on the books is another way in which states attempt to discourage the related crime of fornication.

Can the existence of a law prohibiting cohabitation affect an unmarried person's rights in other areas?

Yes. In a recent case,[8] a police officer had been dismissed from the force for cohabiting out of wedlock in a state that did not have an anticohabitation statute. He then brought a civil rights action against the police department, alleging that his constitutional right to privacy had been violated. The court found in the plaintiff officer's favor, holding that the department had infringed on his constitutional right to sexual privacy. The court noted that the officer had not violated a state statute barring lewd and lascivious conduct, but rather merely was unmarried and cohabiting, an act insufficient to violate state criminal law. Thus, the fact that the officer's cohabitation was not punishable under state law had a direct bearing on his right to maintain an action to recover for unconstitutional employment discrimination.[9]

What is "fornication"?

Fornication is heterosexual intercourse between persons who are not husband and wife.

Is fornication a crime?

Yes, in thirteen states and the District of Columbia. The states in which fornication is a crime are Florida, Georgia, Idaho, Illinois, Massachusetts, Mississippi, North Carolina, North Dakota, Rhode Island, South Carolina, Utah, Virginia, and West Virginia.[10]

Do fornication statutes all proscribe the same conduct?

No. Some of these statutes have special provisions. In Georgia and in Washington, D.C., for example, at least one of the participants must be unmarried. In North Dakota, the act of fornication must have been committed in a public place.[11] And in Wisconsin, which has repealed its basic law against fornication, fornication is still a crime if committed (a) with a person between sixteen and eighteen years of age who is not the other's spouse; or (b) in public.[12] These variations highlight the importance of consulting the specific state statute in the event you have a problem.

Do fornication laws apply only to unmarried persons?

Not entirely. In Illinois, a married or unmarried person

can commit the crime by having intercourse with another person who is not his or her spouse. In Florida, the offense must involve an unmarried woman. But in Georgia, only an unmarried person may commit the offense; and in Idaho fornication occurs only when two unmarried persons have sexual intercourse.[13] Of course, *no* fornication statute applies to sexual intercourse if engaged in by persons who are husband and wife.

What is the origin of fornication laws?

Fornication was punished in the earliest colonies. In fact, 210 of the 370 criminal prosecutions in colonial Massachusetts were for fornication.[14] A commentator reports a "steady succession of trials and convictions for sexual offenses involving single persons" in Plymouth Colony.[15]

Are laws prohibiting fornication and cohabitation permissible under the Constitution?

Laws prohibiting fornication and cohabitation are not explicitly forbidden by the Constitution. And though certain Justices have indicated that states may regulate private, consensual sex among adults,[16] the Supreme Court has reserved judgment on the question.[17]

Can a person accused of fornication or cohabitation argue that the statute violates his or her constitutional rights?

Yes. There are several arguments that can be marshaled against the constitutionality of laws prohibiting fornication and cohabitation. At the heart of the matter is the question whether single persons share the right to privacy that inheres in the marital relationship. In one important case, in which the Supreme Court extended to unmarried persons the right to use contraceptives,[18] the Court stated that

> ... the marital couple is not an independent entity with a mind and heart of its own, but an association of two individuals each with a separate intellectual and emotional makeup. If the right of privacy means anything it is the right of the individual, married or single, to be free from unwarranted governmental intrusion into matters so fundamentally affecting a

person as the decision whether to bear or beget a child.[19]

While this may sound encouraging, it is not a holding to the effect that single persons share married couples' rights with respect to all matters affecting sexual privacy.

What are some of the arguments available to a litigant challenging the constitutionality of laws prohibiting fornication and cohabitation?

Among the arguments available to those who would challenge these laws are—

1. that sexual acts are so intimate and personal that they could be discovered only through unlawful intrusion into a single person's protected zone of privacy;

2. that the home is a sanctuary and that where, within it, acts occur that do not harm others, the government may not intrude;

3. that every person has the right to associate and live with a sexual partner of one's choice, without interference from the government;

4. that every person has the right to familial privacy, and that cohabitation is a modern, functional equivalent of a family unit;

5. that every person has the freedom to marry (and by extension, not to marry).[20]

These rights, if applied by a court to a single person, would then have to be weighed against the state's interests in outlawing fornication and cohabitation.

What are the state's interests in preventing fornication and cohabitation?

Reasons offered for these laws are (1) the prevention of illegitimacy; (2) the preservation of the family; (3) the promotion of public health (by the prevention of venereal disease—a blood test is required prior to marriage); and (4) the enforcement of morality. Each of these may be questioned. Clearly there are more effective ways of preventing illegitimacy and venereal disease. Indeed, no fornication or cohabitation statute distinguishes between nonmarital liaisons that produce children and those that do not. None of these statutes addresses directly the purported concern for public health, nor does any state proscribe marital sexual conduct that might produce venereal disease. The true underlying purpose appears to be coercion toward the marital state. Regarding the morality argument, a leading spokesman for law as an expression of morality in Victorian England wrote as follows:

> A law which enters into a direct contest with a fierce imperious passion, which the person who feels it does not admit to be bad, and which is not directly injurious to others, will generally do more harm than good; and this is perhaps the principle reason why it is impossible to legislate directly against unchastity unless it takes forms which every one regards as monstrous and horrible.[21]

Has any state court ruled that a fornication statute is unconstitutional?

Courts in Florida, Iowa, and New Jersey have so ruled.[22] In both Iowa and New Jersey, the courts ruled that the fornication law as applied to private, consensual intercourse between adults of the opposite sex infringed on the individual's right to privacy. The Florida court invalidated the fornication law on its face, under both the United States and Florida constitutions, on the ground that it impermissibly disguished between married men and married women (who under the Florida law could not commit the crime at all).

Is there a trend toward the legislative repeal of fornication statutes?

Since 1975, Alabama, Alaska, California, Indiana, Nebraska, and Wisconsin[23] have repealed fornication statutes.

One reason for repeal has been stated by two commentators.

> The law against fornication, when it has not been repealed, has fallen into decline, withering away under the impact of mass, open defiance, lack of prosecution and enforcement, a complete absence of

public support, and apathy toward the law (including
ignorance of it) on the part of the violators.[24]

Even where fornication laws still are on the books, like
statutes barring cohabitation, they are not aggressively enforced in most jurisdictions.

Can the existence of criminal statutes prohibiting fornication affect any other rights of the individual?

Yes. There is a New York case in which a landlord sought
eviction of a female tenant based on her alleged private,
noncommercial fornication on the premises.[25] New York had a
rent regulation that permitted eviction based on the use of
the premises for any "immoral or illegal purpose." Assuming
that the regulation itself was valid, the trial judge examined
the alleged conduct and determined that New York had no
law barring private, nonmarital, consensual, noncommercial
sex. That resolved the legality question. Moreover, in dismissing
the landlord's morality argument, the judge observed that the
state did not criminalize the alleged conduct. Thus, he decided that no basis existed for eviction.[26]

Is sexual conduct regulated by any federal law?

Yes. Although states have the primary responsibility for
regulating criminal sexual conduct, one federal law merits
comment—the Mann Act.[27] This statute prohibits the know-
ing transportation in interstate or foreign commerce of "any
woman or girl . . . for any . . . immoral purpose, or with the
intent and purpose to induce, entice, or compel such woman
or girl to . . . engage in any . . . immoral practice." In addition,
the statute proscribes the procurement of tickets for transportation for the prohibited purpose. The statute also reaches
intentional persuasion or enticement of a woman or girl

> to go from one place to another in interstate or
> foreign commerce . . . for any . . . immoral purpose,
> or with the intent and purpose on the part of such
> person that such woman or girl shall engage in . . .
> any . . . immoral practice, whether with or without
> her consent, and thereby knowingly causes such
> woman or girl to go and to be carried or transported
> as a passenger

by a common carrier in interstate commerce. The punishment is $5,000 and/or up to 5 years in a federal prison. This statute is primarily aimed at the transport of prostitutes, and is rarely enforced against persons who engage in private, isolated, noncommercial acts of sexual intercourse, even if they cross state lines to do it.

What is "adultery"?

At common law, *adultery* was defined as sexual intercourse by a man, married or single, with a married woman not his wife. Thus, at common law, an unmarried woman could not commit the crime of adultery. Now adulterous conduct is regulated by statute, and the definition of the crime varies with the jurisdiction. In general, adultery is sexual intercourse between two persons, at least one of whom is married, but who are not married to one another.

Who can be convicted for committing adultery?

It depends on the state. The following states punish both the unmarried and married partners to an adulterous liaison: Alabama, Arizona, Florida, Idaho, Illinois, Kansas, Maryland, Massachusetts, Mississippi, New Hampshire, New York, North Carolina, Oklahoma, Rhode Island, South Carolina, West Virginia, and Wisconsin.[28] Michigan, adhering to the common law definition, punishes anyone except an unmarried woman,[29] as does the District of Columbia.[30] Laws against adultery apply only to married persons in Colorado, Connecticut, Georgia, North Dakota, Nebraska, Utah, and Virginia.[31]

Is adultery permitted in any state?

Yes. Adulterous relationships are not proscribed in Alaska, Arkansas, Delaware, Indiana, Iowa, Kentucky, Louisiana, Maine, Minnesota, Missouri, Montana, New Jersey, New Mexico, Ohio, Oregon, South Dakota, Tennessee, Texas, Vermont, Washington, and Wyoming. It should be noted that several of these states punish adultery if it is incestuous. In other words, if two people have sexual intercourse, and if their marriage would be void for incest, then they could be punished for fornication or adultery. This is true in California, Nevada, and Vermont.[32]

What is the origin of adultery laws?

In England, centuries ago, the crime of adultery was exclusively within the jurisdiction of the ecclesiastical courts, following the prohibition contained in the Seventh Commandment, Exodus 20:14.[33] Cromwell initiated secular punishment, but this was abandoned after the Restoration. The Puritans reinstated it. By 1954, in this country, 30 states punished adultery (4 only imposed a fine).[34]

What is the present trend?

There is a trend toward the repeal of these laws. Within the last ten years, several states, including New Jersey, Texas, Vermont, and Washington, have repealed laws prohibiting adultery. And even the laws that exist are rarely enforced.[35]

Are adultery statutes constitutional?

Yes. Earlier decisions and at least one recent court have upheld adultery statutes against constitutional challenge. In the recent case, two adults, each married but not to the other, were prosecuted for having had intercourse in a van in a secluded, wooded area. In defense they claimed that under the Constitution they had a right to privacy that would protect the conduct. The court held that there is "no fundamental personal privacy right . . . barring the prosecution of consenting adults committing adultery in private."[36] The court upheld the state's interest in protecting the marital relationship, holding that the state could prohibit conduct that threatens marriage. Thus, the adultery law in question was a "permissible expression of public policy."

Is there any nonconstitutional defense to a charge of adultery?

Yes, in certain circumstances a defendant may claim that the spouse of the partner condoned the act. The defense of condonation may consist of proof of "forgiveness" of a prior act of adultery. However, such forgiveness contains an implied condition that the conduct will not be repeated and that the errant spouse will treat the offended spouse with "conjugal kindness."[37] If extramarital sexual activity occurs after the offending spouse has been forgiven, the condonation defense is ineffective.[38]

What is the Model Penal Code position on fornication and adultery?

The Model Penal Code, which is formulated by the American Law Institute (ALI), does not include the crimes of fornication and adultery.[39] A number of reasons contributed to this decision. The ALI found that fornication and adultery statutes are rarely enforced, notwithstanding that adulterers are easily identified in that adultery is a judicial ground for divorce. Moreover, the ALI warned against the misuse of such "dead letter" laws. The danger of these statutes is that they will be enforced selectively against minorities or political figures and that their prosecution will involve surveillance that would jeopardize the delicate relationship between the individual and the state. Furthermore, the ALI found that fornication and adultery laws were often levers for blackmail and extortion, and could breed disrespect for the criminal law. Finally, the ALI found that enforcement of community morality is an insufficient reason to proscribe private, consensual sexual conduct, and noted that the trend toward no-fault divorces undercuts the need to proscribe adulterous conduct in order to secure an otherwise unhappy marriage. The authors of the code suggested that, since prosecutorial resources were limited, they should be allocated to the prosecution of more dangerous activities.

What is "sodomy"?

Sodomy is deviate sexual intercourse. In early English law it was defined narrowly as copulation per anum. In most American jurisdictions it includes anal and oral intercourse.[40] In criminal statutes, it is referred to variously as—

1. the crime against nature;[41]
2. the infamous crime against nature;[42]
3. the abominable and detestable crime against nature;[43]
4. deviate sexual activity;[44]
5. the unnatural and lascivious act;[45]
6. the abominable crime of buggery.[46]

Generally, sodomy refers to homosexual relationships, although, by definition, many of the statutory proscriptions can apply to heterosexual sex. This discussion of sodomy does not include acts involving force, minors, or bestiality.

What is the origin of sodomy laws?

According to Leviticus 20:13, "And if a man also lie with mankind, as with womankind, both of them have committed abomination: they shall surely be put to death; their blood shall be upon them." This religious proscription was adopted in the Laws of the Colony of New York. "If a man lyeth with mankind as he lyeth with a woman, they shall be put to death. . . ."[47]

Do sodomy laws discriminate against single persons?

Yes. Sodomy laws, for the most part, are directed to homosexual activity. As such, they are treated in depth in the ACLU handbook, *The Rights of Gay People*,[48] but have implications for unmarried persons who are not homosexual as well.

In prohibiting deviate sexual activity, do sodomy laws distinguish between married and unmarried persons?

Most of the twenty-five states that proscribe sodomy do not distinguish on the basis of marital status, but Alabama and Kentucky exclude married couples from this prohibition.[49] However, courts in New York and Pennsylvania have declared that laws barring sodomy only between unmarried persons are unconstitutional.[50] Five states make a distinction based on sexual preference by proscribing deviate sexual activity only when practiced by homosexuals: Arkansas, Kansas, Montana, Nevada, and Texas.[51] Though these statutes focus their discrimination on gays, the homosexual/heterosexual distinction is relevant for single persons in that gay partners cannot marry one another.[52]

Is there presently a trend toward decriminalizing private acts of sodomy by consenting adults?

Yes. During the last fourteen years, the following states have decriminalized such acts: Alaska (1980), California (1976), Colorado (1971), Connecticut (1971), Delaware (1973), Hawaii (1973), Illinois (1972), Indiana (1977), Iowa (1978), Maine (1976), Nebraska (1978), New Hampshire (1973), New Mexico (1975), North Dakota (1977), Ohio (1974), Oregon (1972), South Dakota (1977), Vermont (1977), Washington (1976), West Virginia (1976), and Wyoming (1977).[53]

Are sodomy laws constitutional?

Probably, although the United States Supreme Court has not yet answered this question.[54] Several states have upheld consensual sodomy laws against a privacy attack.[55] However, at least two state courts have held sodomy laws to be unconstitutional as violations of the right to privacy.[56] Sodomy statutes have been challenged on vagueness grounds as well (that is, the statute does not give sufficient notice of what acts are prohibited). In fourteen jurisdictions, challenges to sodomy laws have been upheld against challenges based on vagueness.[57] Courts in Ohio and Florida invalidated statutes because of vagueness, then upheld slightly less vague, redrafted ones.[58] The United States Supreme Court twice has upheld state sodomy laws against vagueness challenges.[59]

What is the punishment for sodomy conviction?

It can be harsh. A convicted defendant can be imprisoned for 20 years (Arizona, Georgia, or Rhode Island), 17 years (Michigan), 15 years (Tennessee), 5 years at hard labor (Louisiana), or a maximum of 10 years (Alabama, Maryland, Mississippi, Montana, Nevada, and Oklahoma). In Michigan a convicted defendant can receive life imprisonment if found to be a "sexually delinquent person"; in North Carolina the defendant may be imprisoned at the discretion of the court.[60] This opens another possible constitutional challenge, under the cruel and unusual punishment provision of the Eighth Amendment. Possible lines of attack are the disproportionate severity of the sentence versus the sentences of people who committed more serious crimes in the same jurisdiction or the same offense in another jurisdiction.

Can a divorced, now single, woman press charges against a former husband for rape or sexual assault?

Yes. Though there exists in some states a spousal exemption from prosecution for rape or sexual assault, the exemption does not apply when the victim is not married to the aggressor. This distinction may be relevant not only to single women but to women en route to dissolving a marriage, a time when many sexual assault cases arise. Thus, even in some states that honor the spousal exemption, immunity from prosecution disappears at various points along the continuum toward divorce.

In the following ten states the exemption exists only until a decree of separation has been issued: Kentucky, Louisiana, Maryland, Montana, North Carolina, North Dakota, Pennsylvania, South Carolina, Utah, and Wyoming.[61] The Model Penal Code adopts this approach.[62] Eight states apply the exemption until an action for divorce has been filed: Indiana, Michigan, Minnesota, Nevada, Rhode Island, Tennessee, Washington, and Wisconsin.[63] In five states the immunity vanishes once the parties are living apart: Alaska, Colorado, Idaho, Iowa, and New Mexico.[64]

Can an unmarried woman obtain a protective order against a cohabitant who threatens her with sexual violence?

In some states, yes. The Minnesota legislature recently passed a law authorizing a court to issue a protective order against domestic abuse by a former spouse *or by others*.[65] This is an important development in that it extends to single women a right that traditionally has been reserved for married women.

In a related development, Washington State has passed a domestic violence statute whose explicit purpose is to assure victims maximum protection of the law. The legislature, recognizing the historical difference in its treatment of unmarried women, stressed enforcement to protect the victim *without regard to marital status*.[66] Under this approach, in attempting to reduce domestic violence, local police more likely will extend to unmarried women efforts that otherwise may have been limited to threatened wives.

In a recent case in Oregon, that state's highest court ruled that a woman could sue a police officer for failing to enforce a protective order entered for her benefit. The order had been entered pursuant to Oregon's Abuse Prevention Act, which had been enacted to strengthen legal protection for persons threatened with assault by a present or former spouse or cohabitant. In enforcing the act the Oregon court held that, where a police officer knowingly failed to enforce a judicial order entered to benefit a threatened spouse or cohabitant, the officer could be liable for the resulting physical or emotional harm to the threatened person.[67]

But the trend toward equalizing the treatment of married and unmarried women with respect to crimes of domestic sexual violence cuts both ways. Texas has passed a law that extends to cohabitants the exemption from prosecution for interspousal violence. The law "extends to conduct of persons while cohabiting, regardless of the legal status of their relationship and of whether they hold themselves out as husband and wife."[68] In the commentary, the legislature has explained that "[a]dults cohabiting may terminate their relationship if one dislikes the other's sexual conduct and there is no justification for the criminal law's intrusion into their relationship."[69] Thus, while similar to the Washington approach in its equalization of married and unmarried partners, the Texas provision serves to immunize cohabitants from prosecution for otherwise criminal conduct.

May marital status affect decisions involving bail, probation, and parole?

Yes. Marital status is relevant not only in the definition of crimes, but also in how accused persons are treated. In determining whether a defendant will be released on bail, for example, it is common for courts to consider, among other things, the accused's family ties, including his or her marital status. This is codified in the federal bail statute.[70]

States follow the same course. Thus, where bail is discretionary, a judge must consider family ties in determining the degree of risk presented by the bail applicant.[71] Some states codify this consideration, directing courts to consider family ties in disposing of bail applications.[72]

Family status may also affect probation, parole, and parole revocation decisions. Thus, close family ties may help to persuade corrections officials to release a person who has been in custody. The theory is that the strength of the family tie will keep the person out of trouble (or in the case of bail, will ensure his or her return to court). Consideration of family ties does not necessarily disadvantage a single person in that strong family ties may exist outside of the marital relationship. In addition, defendants and prisoners who have strong nonfamily relationships can argue that such relationships will serve the same beneficial purpose.

NOTES

1. This crime is often referred to as lewd (Idaho) or lewd and lascivious (West Virginia) cohabitation. For statutory cites, *see* note 2.
2. ALA. CODE §13A–13–2 (included within the adultery laws); ARIZ. REV. STAT. ANN. §13–1409; FLA. STAT. §798.02; IDAHO CODE §18–6604; ILL. ANN. STAT. ch. 38, §11–8; MASS. ANN. LAWS ch. 272, §16; MICH. COMP. LAWS §750.335; MISS. CODE ANN. §97–29–1; N.M. STAT. ANN. §30–10–2; N.D. CENT. CODE §12.1–20–10; S.C. CODE ANN. §16–15–60 (included within the fornication statute); VA. CODE §18.2–345; W. VA. CODE §61–8–4.
3. ALA. CODE §13A–13–2.
4. *See, e.g.,* Wisconsin Act 17, §7 (1983).
5. *See, e.g.,* FLA. STAT. §798.02 (to 60 days; to $500); MASS. ANN. LAWS ch. 272, §16 (to 3 years; to $300); MICH. COMP. LAWS §750.335 (to 1 year; to $500); MISS. CODE ANN. §97–29–1 (to 6 months; to $500); VA. CODE §18.2–345 ($500 fine).
6. Note, "Fornication, Cohabitation and the Constitution," 77 *Mich. L. Rev.* 252, 254 n.8 (1978).
7. *Id.*
8. *Briggs v. North Muskegon Police Dep't.,* 563 F. Supp. 585 (W.D. Mich. 1983).
9. Federal courts are divided over the question whether sexual conduct outside marriage is protected by the Constitution. Some courts have held that the Constitution does not protect such conduct. *See, e.g., Baron v. Meloni,* 556 F. Supp. 796 (W.D.N.Y. 1983); *Suddarth v. Slane,* 539 F. Supp. 612 (W.D. Va. 1982); *Johnson v. San Jacinto Jr. College,* 498 F. Supp. 555 (S.D. Tex. 1980) (adulterous relationship is not protected by the Constitution); *Wilson v. Swing,* 463 F. Supp. 555 (M.D.N.C. 1978); *Hollenbaugh v. Carnegie Free Library,* 436 F. Supp. 1328 (W.D. Pa. 1977), *cert. denied,* 439 U.S. 1052 (1978). But other courts have joined with *Briggs, supra* note 8, in holding that the Constitution does protect such conduct. *See, e.g., Baker v. Wade,* 553 F. Supp. 1121 (N.D. Tex. 1982); *Shuman v. City of Philadelphia,* 470 F. Supp. 449 (E.D. Pa. 1979); *Smith v. Price,* 446 F. Supp. 828 (M.D. Ga. 1977), *rev'd on other grounds,* 616 F.2d 1371 (5th Cir. 1980); *People v. Onofre,* 415 N.E.2d 936 (N.Y. 1980), *cert. denied,* 451 U.S. 987 (1981).
10. FLA. STAT. §798.03; GA. CODE ANN. §26–2010; IDAHO CODE §18–6603; ILL. ANN. STAT., ch. 38, §11–8; MASS. ANN. LAWS, ch. 272, §18; MISS. CODE ANN. §97–29–1; N.C. GEN. STAT. §14–184; N.D. CENT. CODE §12.1–20–08 (contains the requirement that the act be commit-

ted in a public place); R.I. GEN. LAWS §11–6–3; S.C. CODE 16–15–60; UTAH CODE ANN. §76–7–104; VA CODE §18.2–344; W. VA. CODE §61–8–3. The District of Columbia citation is D.C. CODE §22–1002.

11. *See* statutory cites, *supra* note 10.

12. WIS. STAT. ANN. §944.15 and Act 17, §4 (1983).

13. *See* statutory cites, *supra* note 10.

14. Note, *supra* note 6, at 253.

15. *Id.* [citing Nelson, "Emerging Notions of Modern Criminal Law in the Revolutionary Era," 43 *NYU L. Rev.* 450, 452 (1967)].

16. *See Paris Adult Theatre I v. Slaton*, 413 U.S. 49, 68 (1973); *Griswold v. Connecticut*, 381 U.S. 479, 498 (1965).

17. *Carey v. Population Services International*, 431 U.S. 678, 688 n.5, 694 n.17 (1977).

18. *Eisenstadt v. Baird*, 405 U.S. 438, 447 (1972).

19. *Id.* at 453.

20. *See generally* Note, *supra* note 6, at 272 *et seq*.

21. *Id.* [quoting J. Stephen, *Liberty, Equality, Fraternity* (1837)].

22. *Purvis v. State*, 377 So. 2d 674 (Fla. 1979); *State v. Pilcher*, 242 N.W.2d 348 (Iowa 1976); *State v. Saunders*, 381 A.2d 333 (N.J. 1977).

23. ALA. CODE §13A–13–2 (omits fornication, with a commentary regarding the difficulty of enforcement and noting the fact that in many other states, fornication is not a crime); ALASKA STAT. §11.40.040 (repealed effective, Jan. 1, 1980 by ch. 166, §21, 1978 ALASKA SESS. LAWS 219); CAL. PENAL CODE §269a (repealed by ch. 71, §5, 1975 CAL. STAT. 131); IND. CODE §35–1–82–2 (repealed by Pub. L. No. 148, 24, 1976 Ind. Acts 718); NEB. REV. STAT. §28–928 (repealed by Legislative Bill 38, §328, 1977 NEB. LAWS 88); WIS STAT. ANN. §944.15.

24. D. MacNamara and E. Sagarin, *Sex, Crime and the Law* 187 (1977). *See also* Note, *supra* note 6, at 271.

25. *Edwards v. Roe*, 327 N.Y.S.2d 307 (N.Y. Civ. Ct. 1971).

26. *Id.*

27. 18 U.S.C. §§2421, 2422.

28. ALA. CODE §13A–13–2; ARIZ. REV. STAT. ANN. §13–1–408; FLA. STAT. §798.01; IDAHO CODE §18–6601; KAN. STAT. ANN. §21–3507; ILL. ANN. STAT. §11–7 (the defendant must know that his partner is married); MD. ANN. CODE art. 27, §4 ($10 fine); MASS. ANN. LAWS ch. 272, §14; MISS CODE ANN. §97–29–1; N.H. REV. STAT. ANN. §645:3 (knowledge of the partner's marital status is required); N.Y. PENAL LAW §155.17 (a reasonable belief that the partner is unmarried is a defense); N.C. GEN. STAT. §14–184 (1981). *See also Nicholson v. Hugh Chatham Mental Hospital*, 266 S.E.2d 818 (N.C. 1980); OKLA. STAT. ANN. tit. 21, §871 (up to 5 years in prison); R.I. GEN. LAWS §11–6–2; S.C. CODE ANN. §16–15–70; W. VA. CODE §61–8–3; WIS. STAT. ANN. §944.16.

29. MICH. COMP. LAWS §750.30.
30. D.C. CODE §22–301.
31. COLO. REV. STAT. §18–6–501; CONN. GEN. STAT. ANN. §53a–81; GA. CODE ANN. §16–6–19; NEB. REV. STAT. §28–704 (adultery includes anal and oral intercourse and includes a requirement of cohabitation); N.D. CENT. CODE §12.1–20.09; UTAH CODE ANN. §76–7–103; VA. CODE §18.2–365 (1982). In Georgia, adultery includes extramarital homosexual as well as heterosexual conduct. *See Owens v. Owens*, 274 S.E.2d 484 (Ga. 1981).
32. CAL. PENAL CODE §285; NEV. REV. STAT. §201.180; VT. STAT. ANN. tit. 13, §205.
33. *See also* Leviticus 20:10; Deuteronomy 22:22.
34. American Law Institute, Model Penal Code, art. 213, at 430–31 (1980).
35. *Id. See also Commonwealth v. Stowell*, 449 N.E.2d 357, 360–61 (Mass. 1983).
36. *Commonwealth, supra* note 35, at 360.
37. *Tigert v. Tigert*, 595 P.2d 815 (Okla. 1979).
38. *Bourlon v. Bourlon*, 9 Fam. L. Rptr. (BNA) (Okla. Oct. 4, 1983).
39. MODEL PENAL CODE, art. 213, at 430–39 (1980).
40. *See generally* Note, *"Commonwealth v. Bonadio:* Voluntary Deviate Sexual Intercourse—A Comparative Analysis," 43 U. Pitt. L. Rev. 253 (1981).
41. ALA. CODE §13–1–110; ARIZ. REV. STAT. ANN. §13–1411; LA. REV. STAT. ANN. §14.89; N.C. GEN. STAT. §14–17; TENN. CODE ANN. §39–707.
42. IDAHO CODE §18–6605; NEV. REV. STAT. §201.190.
43. MASS. GEN. LAWS ANN. ch. 272. §§34, 35; MICH. COMP. LAWS ANN. §750.158; MISS. CODE ANN. §97–29–59; OKLA. STAT. ANN. tit. 21, §886; R.I. GEN. LAWS §11–10–1.
44. KY. REV. STAT. ANN. §510.100; MONT. CODE ANN. §45–5–505; TEX. PENAL CODE ANN. tit. 5, §21.06.
45. FLA. STAT. ANN. §800.02.
46. S.C. CODE ANN. §16–15–120.
47. Code of the Duke of New York, Laws of the Colony of New York (1665). *See also* Katz, "Sexual Morality and the Constitution: *People v. Onofre*," 46 *Albany L. Rev.* 311–62 (1982).
48. ACLU Handbook, *The Rights of Gay People*, by E. Boggan, M. Haft, C. Lister, J. Rupp & T. Stoddard (1983), at 108–18.
49. ALA. CODE §13A–6–60(2); KY. REV. STAT. §510.010.
50. *Onofre, supra* note 9; *Commonwealth v. Bonadio*, 415 A.2d 47 (Pa. 1980).
51. ARK. STAT. ANN. §41–1813; KAN. STAT. ANN. §21–3505; MONT. CODE ANN. §94–5–505; NEV. REV. STAT. §201.190; TEX. PENAL CODE ANN. tit. 5 §21.06.

52. ACLU Handbook, *supra* note 48, at 81.

53. *See* Rivera, "On Straight-Laced Judges: The Legal Position of Homosexuals in the United States," 30 *Hastings L. J.* 799–955 (1979).

54. *See supra* note 17. There are dicta in United States Supreme Court decisions to the effect that states may, consistent with the Constitution, criminalize nonmarital sexual conduct, including homosexual conduct. *See Griswold, supra* note 16, at 498–99 (Goldberg, J., concurring). *See also Poe v. Ullman*, 367 U.S. 497, 553 (1960) (Harlan, J., dissenting).

55. *See, e.g., State v. McCoy*, 337 So. 2d 192 (La. 1976); *Kelly v. State*, 412 A.2d 1274 (Md. 1980); *People v. Coulter*, 288 N.W.2d 448 (Mich. 1980); *State v. Santos*, 413 A.2d 58 (R.I. 1980).

56. *Pilcher, supra* note 22; *Onofre, supra* note 9. In a companion statute, New York had also prohibited loitering in a public place to engage in or solicit deviate sex, N.Y. PENAL LAW §240.35(3). In the wake of *Onofre, supra* note 9, the New York Court of Appeals, the highest court in the state of New York, invalidated the loitering statute on the grounds that the underlying act was lawful if committed in private by consenting adults. *People v. Uplinger*, 447 N.E.2d 62 (N.Y. 1983) *cert. gr.*, 104 S.Ct. 64 (1983), *cert. dism'd.*, 140 S.Ct. 2332 (1984).

57. *See* Note, *supra* note 40, at 271 n.141.

58. *See* Katz, *supra* note 47, at 312.

59. *Rose v. Locke*, 423 U.S. 48 (1975); *Wainwright v. Stone*, 414 U.S. 21 (1973).

60. The statutory citations for the punishments identified are, respectively: ARIZ. REV. STAT. ANN. §13–1411; GA. CODE ANN. §26–2002; R.I. GEN. LAWS §11–10–1; MICH. COMP. LAWS ANN. §750.158; TENN. CODE ANN. §39–707; LA. REV. STAT. ANN. §14:89; ALA. CODE §13–1–110; MD. ANN. CODE art. 27, §§553, 554; MISS. CODE ANN. §97–29–59 (1972); MONT. CODE ANN. §45–5–505; NEV. REV. STAT. §201.190; OKLA. STAT. ANN. tit. 21, §886; N.C. GEN. STAT. §14–177.

61. KY. REV. STAT. §510.010(3); LA. REV. STAT. ANN. §14–41; MD. CRIM. LAW CODE ANN. §464(d); MONT. CODE ANN. §94–5–506(2); N.C. GEN. STAT. §14–27.8; N.D. CENT. CODE §12.1–20–01(2); 18 PA. CONS. STAT. §3103; S.C. CODE ANN. §16–3–658; UTAH CODE ANN. §76–5–407; WYO. STAT. §6–4–307.

62. MODEL PENAL CODE §213.6(2) (1956).

63. IND. CODE §35–42–4–1(b); MICH. STAT. ANN. §750.520; MINN. STAT. §609.349; NEV. REV. STAT. §200.373; R.I. GEN. LAWS §11–37–1; TENN. CODE ANN. §39–3709; WASH. REV. CODE ANN. §§9A.44.010(2), 9A.44.040 (must also be living apart); WIS. STAT. §940.225(6).

64. ALASKA STAT. §11.45.445(1); COLO. REV. STAT. §18–3–409(2); IDAHO CODE §18–6107(2); IOWA CODE §709.4; N.M. STAT. ANN. §30–9–10(E).

65. Minnesota S.B. 240 (chap. 52). This development is reported in 9 Fam. L. Rptr. (BNA) 2475 (June 7, 1983).

66. WASH. REV. CODE ANN. §10.99.010 (1979).

67. *Nearing v. Weaver*, 670 P.2d 137, 138–39 (Or. 1983).
68. Tex. Penal Code §21.12.
69. *Id.*
70. 18 U.S.C. §3146.
71. *See, e.g., In re Podesto*, 544 P.2d 1297 (Cal. 1976).
72. *See, e.g.*, N.Y. Crim. Proc. Law §510.30(2)(a)(iii).

III.
Housing

Can municipalities adopt zoning ordinances that restrict the rights of single people to choose with whom they prefer to live?

Yes, in most states. In 1974, in the case *Village of Belle Terre v. Boraas*, the United States Supreme Court upheld a local ordinance that prohibited the occupancy of any dwelling by more than two unrelated persons even though the same ordinance allowed the occupancy of any number of persons related to each other by blood, marriage, or adoption.[1] The ordinance was challenged by a home owner and by the several unrelated students to whom he had rented his dwelling. The tenants argued that the ordinance violated their constitutional rights of privacy and freedom of association. The Supreme Court rejected this argument and affirmed the right of government to promote "traditional family life" through its zoning authority.[2]

Several years after the Supreme Court affirmed *Belle Terre*'s ordinance, it held, in *Moore v. City of East Cleveland*, that such municipal authority is not without limitation.[3] Inez Moore had been convicted of violating a city ordinance that essentially restricted residency to parents and their children. Ms. Moore's living arrangement—she shared her home with her son and grandchildren—ran afoul of the ordinance because her grandsons were first cousins rather than brothers. The Supreme Court found that the Constitution's protection of "freedom of personal choice in matters of marriage and family life" limited municipal authority.[4] Thus, the Constitution affords protection to those who live in nontraditional or nonnuclear families, so long as each party in the residence is related by blood or adoption. For the rest of the single population, protection—if it exists at all—must come not from the federal Constitution, but rather from state Constitutions.

As the Supreme Court narrows the scope of protection afforded by the Bill of Rights, state courts are increasingly turning to their own Constitutions as sources of affirmative rights.[5] At least two states, New Jersey[6] and California,[7] have justified their refusal to follow the holding of *Belle Terre* by relying on the more expansive protection afforded by their states' Constitutions. Holding that the municipal zoning authority could not be exercised so as to "infringe unnecessarily upon the freedom and privacy of unrelated individuals," the New Jersey Supreme Court declared unconstitutional a local ordinance that limited the right of five or more individuals to live together in a single-family dwelling.[8] The California Supreme Court reached a similar conclusion with regard to a Santa Barbara ordinance. The court held that the privacy clause of the California Constitution was intended to afford protection for "our homes, our families, our thoughts, our emotions, our expressions, our personalities, our freedom of communion, and our freedom to associate with the people we choose."[9]

The Constitutions of at least four other states—Alaska, Hawaii, Illinois, and Louisiana—explicitly guarantee the right of privacy. In these states, municipal ordinances that deprive singles of the right to choose with whom they live might be challenged successfully.

Can single persons who are unrelated by familial or marital bonds ever be considered a family for zoning purposes?

Yes. Notwithstanding the Supreme Court's ruling in *Belle Terre,* a number of state courts have held that their constitutions afford singles protection. Courts in California,[10] Connecticut,[11] Florida,[12] Illinois,[13] Kentucky,[14] New Jersey,[15] New York,[16] and Wisconsin,[17] have insisted that groups of singles who evidence the characteristics of a family unit by their relative permanency are, for purposes of zoning ordinances, the equivalent of biological or legal families. These courts have accepted the principle that municipalities have the right to promote the kind of stable living arrangements traditionally embodied in the family, but have held that "the core concept underlying single family living is not biological or legal relationship, but its character as a single housekeeping unit."[18]

Can a private landlord refuse to rent to a single person because he is single or divorced?

It depends on the state. While there are two important federal laws that prohibit discrimination in housing, neither forbids discrimination on the basis of one's marital status.[19] Thus, there is nothing in federal law to prevent a landlord from refusing to rent to an individual because the person is single or divorced.

Nearly half the states have moved to fill this legal void, outlawing discrimination on the basis of marital status in the rental of housing accommodations (see the Appendix). In these states a landlord or a landlord's agent may not refuse to show or rent housing accommodations to an individual because he is single or divorced. Many of these states, moreover, have created human rights departments that may both investigate, and in some instances adjudicate, allegations of such discrimination.

Can a private landlord refuse to rent to an unmarried couple? Can a landlord evict an unmarried couple because they are cohabiting?

Again it depends on the state. As just discussed, federal law permits landlords to do as they please with regard to cohabitation. In those states that have statutes prohibiting discrimination on the basis of marital status, only three (New Jersey,[20] California,[21] and Washington[22]) have interpreted their statutes so as to allow singles to live together. As a result of the New York Court of Appeals decision in *Hudson View Properties v. Weiss*, there is considerable doubt as to whether similar statutes in the remaining states provide singles sufficient protection.[23]

In the *Weiss* case, Hudson View Properties moved to evict Ms. Weiss shortly after she allowed a man with whom she had developed a "close and loving relationship," to share her apartment. This arrangement, according to the landlord, put Ms. Weiss at odds with her lease, which provided in part that her apartment be occupied only by herself and members of her immediate family. Ms. Weiss, represented by counsel from the New York Civil Liberties Union, took the position that this lease provision violated Section 296(5)(a) of New York State's Human Rights Law, which forbids marital status discrimination in the rental of housing accommodations. The trial court agreed with Ms. Weiss stating:

> The legislative addition of "marital status" to the Human Rights Law reflects the profound changes we have experienced in contemporary mores and the now commonplace practice of unmarried couples establishing households. Although there is little legislative history to guide us, the language of the statute is manifestly clear. This law prohibits landlords from differentiating between those who are married and those who are not married, all other facts being equal. This is precisely what landlord seeks to do. Tenant may continue to reside in her apartment with her companion if they marry. To require that she leave because their relationship lacks the imprimatur of state or benefit of clergy is to terminate her tenancy because of her marital status.[24]

This decision was reversed on appeal. Ignoring the clear legislative history of Section 296(5)(a) and the fact that the New York attorney general had intervened to support the trial court's interpretation, the state's highest court declared that the eviction did not violate the Human Rights Law. According to the court of appeals, Ms. Weiss' living arrangement simply did not comply with her lease. The fact that the individual with whom Ms. Weiss cohabited could become a member of her family by marriage was, in the words of the court, "simply irrelevant."[25]

So great was the public outcry over the *Weiss* decision that, within weeks, the state legislature passed new legislation protecting a tenant's right of cohabitation. Thus, while the New York legislature ultimately provided relief for single tenants in New York, the *Weiss* decision itself sets a precedent in which antidiscrimination laws may be interpreted so as to discriminate against singles. Obviously, if confronted with this situation, you will need to urge the court to adopt the interpretation given the phrase "marital status discrimination" by courts in New Jersey, California, and Washington.[26]

If the cohabiting partner who signed the lease moves out, can the remaining partner stay on in the apartment?

No. Unless the partner is a signatory to the lease, the landlord will be able to evict you. There is one reported decision in New York in which a woman was able to block an eviction after her partner in whose name the lease was signed vacated the apartment.[27] In that instance, the court accepted her argument that since she would have been entitled to remain in the apartment had she been married to the individual who had signed the lease, her eviction would constitute discrimination on the basis of marital status. Unfortunately, the case was decided prior to the New York Court of Appeals's decision in *Weiss*, which held that the state's Human Rights Law did not prevent a landlord from evicting a tenant because of her cohabitation with an individual not a member of her family. Thus, the best way to avoid this problem is by inserting your name on the lease.

Can a person whose name is not on the lease be evicted because he gets divorced?

Yes, if the person's name is not on the lease, unless the lease provides otherwise, or if there is special legislation the landlord may evict.[28] Again, it is always a good idea to have your name on the lease.

Can a private home owner refuse to sell a house to a person because the person is single or divorced?

It depends on the state. The same regulations or lack thereof, that govern landlords apply to home owners. Once again, you must refer to state law because federal law does not prohibit discrimination on the basis of marital status. In states that forbid such discrimination,[29] a refusal to sell because of marital status would clearly be unlawful.

Can a private home owner refuse to sell a house or apartment to an unmarried couple?

Probably. As noted earlier, nothing in federal law prevents this. Moreover, the two cases that have interpreted the scope of protection afforded by state laws forbidding marital status discrimination have gone against the unmarried parties. Both courts that have reviewed the issue have ruled that a refusal to sell to an unmarried *couple* is not an act of marital status discrimination, because only *individuals* have such status.[30] Such tortured reasoning reflects judicial discomfort with cohabitation. Indeed, in the first of these opinions, *McFadden* v. *Elma Country Club,* a Washington court of appeals pointed to a state law criminalizing the cohabitation of nonmarried persons that was in existence at the time of passage of the antimarital status discrimination provision as evidence that the legislature did not intend "marital status discrimination to include discrimination on the basis of a couple's unwed cohabitation."[31] Yet the Washington legislature had in fact abolished such criminal penalties after enacting the marital status discrimination provision, and precisely the opposite conclusion should have been drawn from this "evidence."[32]

The treatment of such evidence appears to be determined by the court's view that cohabitation of unmarried persons is immoral. This is clearer in the second of these opinions, *Prince George's County v. Greenbelt Homes,* where the court boldly asserted that "contemporary discrimination laws are not intended to promulgate promiscuity by favoring relations unrecognized by statute or case law as having legal status."[33] Obviously, to the extent that legislatures by enacting such antidiscrimination statutes meant to "cast aside any prior conceived notion of moral propriety,"[34] these decisions thwart the intent of the people. Unfortunately, the only recourse singles have in the face of such judicial hostility is to petition their elected officials—as was done in New York following the *Weiss* decision—to provide additional protection.

Can single people be excluded from public housing?

Single people are often not eligible to participate in public housing programs, not because these programs specifically exclude them, but because preference is usually given to traditional household units. Federal housing programs for the poor, for example, were originally limited to "families," and the term *family* was limited to two or more people related by blood, marriage, or adoption. The definition of *family* has since been expanded and now includes virtually all singles, but nontraditional households are still placed last on the eligibility lists for federal housing programs, except for the elderly and handicapped.[35] Moreover, by law no more than fifteen percent of the units under the jurisdiction of a public housing agency may be inhabited by single persons.[36]

Can individuals who are divorced or who have had children out of wedlock be excluded from public housing?

No. Individuals who are divorced are treated no differently by the federal regulations than are single persons who have never married. They are therefore subjected to the fifteen-percent limitation. As for individuals with children born out of wedlock, any attempt to bar such individuals on that basis alone would not be supported by the courts.[37]

If a single person is otherwise qualified for low-income housing, can he be evicted for sharing his home or apartment with an individual to whom he is not married?

It depends on the state. While federal regulations allow public housing authorities to evict nonfamily members, such power is circumscribed by state laws forbidding discrimination on the basis of marital status. Thus, in *Atkinson v. Kern Housing Authority*, a California court of appeals held that the eviction of a low-income tenant cohabiting with an unrelated man violated state antidiscrimination laws.[38] But in light of the New York Court of Appeals decision in *Weiss*, the mere existence of state laws forbidding marital status discrimination does not automatically guarantee the result reached in *Atkinson*. Thus, whenever possible, low-income tenants should seek to include within the lease the names of those with whom they wish to live.

If an unmarried couple lives in public housing and the one who qualifies for such housing moves out, can the other stay on?

Federal law defines *families* in part as "the remaining members of a tenant family."[39] Thus, even without being a signatory to the lease, a surviving husband, wife, or child could remain in the apartment. The survivor of a nonmarital relationship is not afforded such protection. Once again, protection for such a single person must come if at all from state law forbidding discrimination on the basis of marital status. *Yorkshire House Assn. v. Lulkin*, while not arising in the subsidized housing context, is the most useful precedent.[40] The remaining tenant was able to block an eviction after her partner (in whose name the lease was signed) vacated the apartment. The court accepted her argument that since she would have been entitled to stay in the apartment had she been married to the lease holder, her eviction would constitute discrimination on the basis of marital status.

Can the federal housing program's preference for "families" be challenged on constitutional due process grounds?

The courts have yet to determine whether such regulations violate the Constitution, but at least one important case suggests that the most blatantly discriminatory schemes do. In 1973, in *U.S. Dept. of Agriculture v. Moreno*,[41] the Supreme Court considered whether unrelated individuals who live together were eligible to participate in the federal food stamp program. Eligibility was based on households, rather than individuals, and the term *household* included only groups whose members were all related to each other (as well as single people living alone). The legislative history of the statute indicated that Congress had defined *household* in this way to exclude "hippies" and "hippie communes" from the food stamp program. The Court voided the restriction because it was "clearly irrelevant to the stated purposes of the Act," which were "to safeguard the health and well-being of the Nation's population and raise levels of nutrition among low-level households." In so doing, the Court stated, "[I]f the constitutional conception of 'equal protection of the laws' means anything, it must at the very least mean that a bare congressional desire to harm a politically unpopular group cannot constitute a 'legitimate' governmental interest."[42]

The Supreme Court's *Belle Terre*[43] decision indicates, however, that the government has the right to promote traditional family life, at least if it does so in a way that is not overly broad or harsh. In that case, the court upheld an ordinance in a suburban community outside New York City that prohibited more than two unrelated people from living together in the same household. According to Justice Douglas's opinion in that case: "The police power is not confined to elimination of filth, stench, and unhealthy places. It is ample to lay out zones where family values, youth values, and the blessings of quiet seclusion and clean air make the area a sanctuary for people."[44]

A more recent case makes clear that *Belle Terre* has its limits; for example, the government may not limit households only to members of the immediate family.[45] Yet *Belle Terre* is still troubling for its suggestion that the government may enact laws that punish or prohibit altogether households that deviate from the traditional mode.

Public Accommodations

Closely related to the issue of discrimination in housing is the treatment of single persons by owners and agents of public accommodations. As is true for housing, neither the Constitution nor federal law prohibits discrimination against single persons in the area of public accommodations. Some thirteen states, however, have outlawed such discrimination (see the Appendix). Although there is no reported case law under these statutes, presumably they would make it illegal to deny a single person a hotel room or service at a bar. It would also be illegal not to afford groups of singles the kinds of discounts afforded married couples by transportation companies and entertainment establishments. To the extent that such statutes were designed to "cast aside any prior conceived notion of moral propriety,"[46] they should also protect the right of an unmarried couple to obtain hotel accommodations.

NOTES

1. *Village of Belle Terre v. Boraas*, 416 U.S. 1 (1974).
2. *Id*. at 7–10.
3. *Moore v. City of East Cleveland*, 431 U.S. 494 (1977).
4. *Id*. at 499.
5. *See generally* Brennan, "State Constitution and the Protection of Individual Rights," 90 *Harv. L. Rev.* 489 (1977).
6. *State v. Baker*, 405 A.2d 368 (N.J. 1979).

7. *City of Santa Barbara v. Adamson*, 610 P.2d 436 (Cal. 1980).

8. *State, supra* note 6, at 372.

9. *City of Santa Barbara, supra* note 7, at 439.

10. *Id.*

11. *Neptune Park Ass'n. v. Steinberg*, 84 A.2d 687 (Conn. 1951).

12. *Carroll v. City of Miami Beach*, 198 So. 2d 643 (Fla. Dist. Ct. App. 1967).

13. *City of Des Plaines v. Trottner*, 216 N.E.2d 116 (Ill. 1966).

14. *Robertson v. Western Baptist Hospital*, 267 S.W.2d 395 (Ky. 1954).

15. *Baker, supra* note 6.

16. *White Plains v. Ferraioli*, 313 N.E.2d 756 (N.Y. 1974).

17. *Missionaries of Our Lady of La Salette v. Village of Whitefish Bay*, 66 N.W.2d 627 (Wis. 1954).

18. *Baker, supra* note 6, at 372.

19. 42 U.S.C. §1982; 42 U.S.C. §§3601 *et seq*.

20. *Zahorian v. Russell Fitt Real Estate Agency*, 301 A.2d 754 (N.J. 1973) (N.J. Stat. Ann. §10:5–12(g) prevents real estate agents from refusing to show an apartment to an individual and her female roommate).

21. *Atkinson v. Kern County Housing Authority*, 130 Cal. Rptr. 375 (Ct. App. 1976) (Civ. Section 51 prevents the Housing Authority from evicting an unwed mother on the grounds that she violated the lease by allowing an adult male to reside with her).

22. *Loveland v. Leslie*, 583 P.2d 664 (Wash. Ct. App. 1978) (Wash. Rev. Code §49.60 prevents landlords from refusing to rent to an individual and his male roommate).

23. *Hudson View Properties v. Weiss*, 450 N.E.2d 234 (N.Y. 1983).

24. 431 N.Y.S.2d 632, 636 (N.Y. Cir. Ct. 1980), *aff'd*, 438 N.Y.S.2d 649 (1982), *rev'd*, 450 N.E.2d 234 (N.Y. 1983).

25. *Hudson View Properties, supra* note 23, at 235.

26. *See supra* notes 20–22.

27. *Yorkshire House Association v. Lulkin*, 450 N.Y.S.2d 962 (N.Y. Civ. Ct. 1982).

28. *See, e.g.*, N.Y.C. Rent Reg. §56 ["No occupant of housing accommodations shall be evicted under this section where the occupant is the surviving spouse of the deceased tenant. Although section 56d speaks of family members of a 'deceased tenant,' the protection has been extended to the family members who lived with a voluntarily vacated primary tenant." *Herzog v. Joy*, 428 N.Y.S.2d 1, 4 (N.Y. App. Div. 1980).]

29. *See* the Appendix for a list of states forbidding marital status discrimination.

30. *See Prince George's County v. Greenbelt Homes*, 431 A.2d 745, 748 (Md. Ct. Spec. App.); *McFadden v. Elma Country Club*, 613 P.2d 146 (Wash. Ct. App. 1980).

31. *McFadden, supra* note 30, at 150.

32. *Id.*

33. *Prince George's County, supra* note 30, at 748.
34. *Hudson View Properties, supra* note 24, at 635.
35. 42 U.S.C. §1437a(3). *See generally The Housing Needs of Non-Traditional Households*, published by the Office of Policy Development and Research of the U.S. Department of Housing and Urban Development (1979).
36. 42 U.S.C. §1437a(3).
37. *Thomas v. Housing Authority of Little Rock*, 282 F. Supp. 575, 580 (E.D. Ark. 1967).
38. *Atkinson, supra* note 21, at 381.
39. 42 U.S.C. §1437(b)(3)(c).
40. *Yorkshire House Association, supra* note 27.
41. *U.S. Dep't of Agriculture v. Moreno*, 418 U.S. 528 (1973).
42. *Id*. at 534.
43. *Village of Belle Terre, supra* note 1, at 1.
44. *Id*. at 9.
45. *Moore, supra* note 3, at 494.
46. *Hudson View Properties, supra* note 24, at 635.

IV.
Employment

Historically, the private employer has had unfettered discretion over employment decisions. Employees have therefore had no recourse against even the most arbitrary or discriminatory actions taken by an employer in regard to hiring, firing, or terms of employment. A major turning point in employer/employee relations occurred in 1964, when Congress passed the Equal Employment Opportunities Act.[1] That act made it unlawful for employers of more than fifteen persons[2] to discriminate on the basis of "race, color, religion, sex or national origin."[3] Intended to protect individuals from being harmed on the basis of characteristics over which they had little or no control, the act offers single persons almost no protection.[4] As a result, to date there is no nationwide protection for single persons seeking employment. Since 1964, however, a number of states have concluded that discrimination based on marital status, like other forms of discrimination, runs counter to the public's interest. At last count, sixteen states plus the District of Columbia prohibit such discrimination (see the Appendix).

In an advertisement soliciting job applicants, can an employer specify a preference for married or single applicants?
It depends on the state. Since the Equal Employment Opportunities Act does not prevent discrimination by employers based on marital status, there is no nationwide prohibition of employment advertising that indicates a preference for married or single persons. However, all of the states listed in

the Appendix, which have made discrimination on the basis of marital status unlawful, prohibit such advertising.

Can an employment agency fill a job request when the employer has asked specifically for either a single or a married person?

Again it depends on the state. Just as employers in most states can discriminate directly against single persons, so too may employment agencies engage in such discrimination on the employer's behalf. However, in states that have barred discrimination in employment neither the employer nor his agent may distinguish between job candidates on the basis of marital status.

Can an employer lawfully inquire into an applicant's marital status or living situation?

Yes. Nothing in federal law prevents such inquiry. Moreover, even in those states that make it unlawful to discriminate on the basis of marital status such inquiry is not absolutely prohibited. Those state laws merely make it an unfair employment practice for an employer to make an inquiry "which expresses directly or indirectly any limitation . . . or intent to make any limitation based on marital status."[5] Notwithstanding the equivocal wording of such statutes, pre-employment inquiry as to one's marital status ought to constitute an unfair labor practice in the states listed in the Appendix.

Can a private employer discriminate against persons in hiring, job assignments, promotions, rates of compensation, or other conditions of employment because they are single?

It depends upon the state in which you live. Because federal law offers single persons no protection, absent state legislation, there is nothing that prohibits an employer from openly discriminating against singles. In those states listed in the Appendix, discrimination against a single person is unlawful. As the New York Court of Appeals stated in *Manhattan Pizza Hut v. New York State Human Rights Appeals Board*, the thrust of these statutes is to "say that employers may no longer decide to hire, fire or promote someone because he or she is single, married, divorced, separated or the like."[6]

May a private employer refuse to hire you, fire you, or otherwise discriminate against you because you are living with someone to whom you are not married?

Again the general rule is that singles are without protection in the employment sector. However, there are a few exceptions to this general rule. First, to the extent that one can show that the employer seeks to regulate the private lives of single women as opposed to single men, an employee may be protected by the Equal Employment Opportunities Act. The Equal Employment Opportunity Commission (EEOC), which is responsible for enforcing the act, has ruled that a company policy barring the employment of unwed mothers constitutes sex discrimination (which as stated earlier is unlawful).[7] There is no reason why this principle would not also prohibit an employer from regulating his female employees' living arrangements even in the absence of pregnancy. Second, even if the employer seeks to regulate the private lives of both male and female employees such conduct is proscribed in those states prohibiting marital status discrimination (see the Appendix).

May a private employer discriminate against a person because he is divorced?

It depends on state law. Such conduct is proscribed by state law forbidding marital status discrimination. Such "statutes in effect say that an employer may no longer decide whether to hire, fire or promote someone because he or she is . . . divorced."[8] However, it should be noted that it is an open question whether state discrimination laws prevent an employer from refusing to hire an individual who had previously been married to someone presently working for the employer. Although the specific question has not been addressed by the courts, the courts are divided over the related question of whether such laws prohibit employers from denying employment to individuals who are married to employees. Courts in Minnesota,[9] Montana,[10] and Washington[11] have held that one's marital status includes the identity of one's spouse and, therefore, an employer may not discriminate against an individual because of the previous employment of the person's spouse. Courts in Michigan,[12] New Jersey,[13] and New York[14] have held that an employer is permitted to turn away an individual because of the party's relationship with another employee. These latter courts reason that the employer's action turns not on the employee's marital status but rather on the employee's particular emotional ties, which disrupt the workplace.

Can a private employer discriminate against an individual because she is an unwed parent?

No. This is the one area in which the Equal Employment Opportunity Act with its nationwide range affords some protection. In 1970, the Equal Employment Opportunity Commission declared unlawful a company policy barring the employment of unmarried parents. The company in question had refused to hire an unwed mother. The commission noted "that bearing a child out of wedlock is a fact not easily hidden from an employer's discovery procedures, whereas it is a wise employer indeed that knows which of its male applicants truthfully answers its illegitimacy inquiry." As a result the commission declared such employer conduct to be a violation of the act's prohibition of sex discrimination.[15] The commission arrived at this conclusion without any finding that a man, if discovered to have fathered a child out of wedlock, would have been retained.

It should be noted, however, that the federal courts, which are responsible for enforcing the EEOC's decisions, are split on the question of whether a finding of sex discrimination can be sustained without actual proof that men and women are treated differently. One federal court of appeals has accepted the EEOC's determination that one need not show that an employer has discharged only unwed mothers to substantiate a claim of sex discrimination as "pregnancy is a condition unique to women, so that termination of employment because of pregnancy has a disparate and invidious impact upon the female gender."[16] Another federal court of appeals, however, has insisted that in order to establish a sex discrimination claim, unwed mothers not offered employment must prove that employers in fact hire unwed fathers.[17]

Can a labor union limit its membership or referrals on the basis of marital status or living situation?

Under federal law, unions may establish any qualification for membership other than race, color, religion, sex, or national origin.[18] Thus in most states unions are free to qualify membership on marital status grounds if they so choose. However, in such a circumstance it would be an unfair labor practice on the part of the employer to refuse to hire an individual who had been denied union membership so long as the individual was willing to tender dues to the union.[19] Moreover, all of the states that have made it unlawful for an employer to discriminate on the basis of marital status have made such provisions applicable to labor organizations. In those states unions may not deny membership on the basis of an individual's marital status.

Can a labor union use its bargaining power to negotiate contracts that discriminate on the basis of marital status or living situation?

No. Under federal law, unions have the power to negotiate with respect to "wages, hours and other terms and conditions of employment."[20] While such terms give unions broad powers, they do not authorize labor organizations to regulate the private lives of employees through bargaining agreements with employers. Furthermore, state antidiscrimination laws specifically forbid such efforts.

Can a union refuse to represent an employee in a grievance that alleges discrimination based on marital status or living situation?

Yes. The Supreme Court of the United States has held that an employee does not have an absolute right to have a grievance taken to arbitration if the union prefers not to.[21] However, at the same time the Court stated that unions are liable for breaching the duty of fair representation owed each worker if the refusal to arbitrate is arbitrary, discriminatory, or in bad faith.[22] In states that forbid discrimination on the basis of marital status, a union's refusal to arbitrate would clearly subject it to liability. Moreover, even in the absence of such state legislation, a strong argument could be made that such a refusal was arbitrary.

Can the federal government discriminate against persons in hiring, job assignments, promotions, rate of compensation, or other conditions of employment because such persons are single or divorced?

Like those states that prohibit discrimination on the basis of marital status, executive agencies of the federal government (with some limited exceptions pertaining to those covering domestic criminal activity or foreign intelligence work) are by statute prohibited from basing employment decisions on whether one is single, married, or divorced.[23] This protection, however, is not afforded employees of the legislative and judicial branches of the federal government. These employees must look to the Constitution for protection.

Can a state or local government discriminate against persons in hiring, job assignments, promotions, rate of compensation, or other conditions of employment because such persons are single or divorced?

Most states do not prohibit such discrimination by their governments. However, to the extent that singles can show that government policies that discriminate against them on the basis of marital status lack a rational basis, the equal protection clause of the Fourteenth Amendment may offer protection.

The equal protection clause requires that any government action or classification be rationally related to a legitimate state end. Thus, in *Andrews v. Drew Municipal School Dist.*, a federal court of appeals struck down a school board policy barring the employment of unwed parents.[24] In that instance the board asserted that its rule was necessary to create a proper moral environment for learning. While the court accepted the legitimacy of such a goal, it found that the board's rule, which was based on a presumption that unwed parents lacked morality, did not rationally further the board's goal.[25]

Federal courts rarely find state policies irrational. A more typical equal protection decision is *Hollenbaugh v. Carnegie Free Library*.[26] Ms. Hollenbaugh had been hired as a librarian by the Carnegie Free Library in December of 1969; two years later the library hired Fred K. Philburn as a janitor. At some point thereafter, they began to see each other socially, even though Mr. Philburn was married. Eventually, when Ms. Hollenbaugh became pregnant as a result of this relationship, the couple decided to live together. Shortly thereafter, they were discharged by the library. In their suit they asserted that as there was no rational connection between their social conduct and their job fitness, the library's action violated the equal protection clause. The library contended, however, that, because this relationship was frowned on by the community, it interfered with the library's ability to serve the public. Finding a rational basis for the library's action, the court was "not willing to call the Board's decision to dismiss an arbitrary, unreasonable, or capricious one."[27] While the added factor of adultery existed in *Hollenbaugh*, the case highlights the fact that "under traditional equal protection analysis a legislative classification must be sustained if the classification is rationally related to a legitimate government interest."[28] In nonlegal parlance this means that singles are not afforded much protection by the equal protection clause.

While a refusal to hire a single person is as much discrimination as a refusal to hire because of race, color, sex, or national origin, taken as a group, singles are by no means a powerless entity in need of special assistance from the courts. The reality, as is witnessed by the legislative actions of sixteen states plus the federal government, is quite the contrary. Should single persons choose to make marital status discrimination legislation a high priority, there is no legal reason why the remaining states could not be brought into line.

Can the federal government, or a state or local government, discriminate against single persons because they are living with someone to whom they are not married, or because they have had children out of wedlock?

While the Constitution does not protect single persons as such, it does protect a person's right to make certain critical life decisions free of government interference. The Supreme Court has deemed marriage,[29] procreation,[30] contraception,[31] abortion,[32] family relationships,[33] child rearing,[34] and family living arrangements[35] so fundamental that they must be left to the individual unless the government can prove a compelling reason for infringement. Based on these opinions, some lower courts have held that a "zone of privacy" protects "a party's private sexual activities . . . from unwarranted government intrusion."[36]

Building on this right of privacy, several federal courts have held that neither school boards nor police departments may penalize single employees for engaging in nonmarital relationships or for cohabiting so long as such conduct does not adversely affect the employee's work.[37] Yet, other courts faced with identical facts have held "that the right to privacy is not unqualified... and that the state has 'more interest in regulating the activities of its employees than the activities of the population at large.'"[38] The Supreme Court has twice declined to hear cases in this area, thereby leaving the scope of the right undefined.[39]

Whatever the scope of the protection ultimately afforded by the Constitution, it should be noted that federal employees already enjoy a statutory right of privacy. By law, no federal employer may "discriminate for or against any employee or applicant for employment on a basis which does not adversely affect the performance of the employee or applicant or the performance of others."[40] Such language can be claimed to protect an employee's nonmarital relationships and/or cohabitation.

Can assignments or promotions in the military be based in part on marital status?

Probably. Although Congress in 1980,[41] repealed the last of several statutes authorizing the discharge of military personnel on marital status grounds, it is highly unlikely that the federal courts would intervene to prevent the military's consideration of one's marital status in decisions about assignment or promotion. This is not because the Constitution is not applicable to the Defense Department,[42] but rather because the level of review concerning action adverse to single persons that the Constitution requires is so minimal. As noted earlier, while the Constitution's due process clause requires that government classifications be rational, federal courts routinely accept any justification offered by the government to prove the rationality of its actions.

Couple this fact with the historical reluctance of the federal judiciary to intervene in military affairs,[43] and it is all but inevitable that matters concerning assignment and promotion within the services are beyond judicial review.

Can the military discriminate against a single person because he is cohabiting with someone?

Probably. A federal court of appeals recently rejected a police officer's claim that it was not within his department's authority to discipline him for living with a woman to whom he was not married. The officer asserted that in discharging him on such grounds, the department violated his constitutional right of privacy. In rejecting the officer's claim, the court stated that it could "ascertain a rational connection between the exigencies of Department discipline and forbidding members of a quasi-military unit to share an apartment or cohabitate."[44] If the courts will allow a small sheriff's department to regulate the private lives of its employees, they will surely pay even greater deference to such regulations by the military.

Can a government security clearance be denied because a person is living with someone to whom he is not married?

Not on that basis alone. All government security clearance programs require that access to classified information be granted only to those whose eligibility is clearly consistent with the national interest.[45] The ultimate determination of whether the nation's interest is served by an individual's clearance is an "overall common sense one based upon all the information which properly may be considered."[46] Courts have been unwilling to sustain challenges to this vague standard.[47]

Can licensing authorities or professional associations consider marital status in deciding whether to grant an individual a license or membership?

No. Authorities that have been granted power by state law to regulate professional membership and standards are treated for constitutional purposes as though they were the state itself. As such, these authorities may not violate the Constitution's equal protection clause. In regard to the licensing of professionals the Supreme Court has stated that any qualification must have a rational connection with the applicant's fitness or capacity to practice the profession.[48] It is difficult to imagine how one's marital status could ever be rationally related to one's ability to engage in professional practice.

Can licensing authorities or professional associations deny a license to an individual because of a single person's nonmarital cohabitation?

Not on that basis alone. Many professional associations

require "good moral character" for admittance and for continuing membership. Such a requirement is constitutionally valid.[49] The mere fact that one resides with another to whom one is not married does not in and of itself substantiate a claim of immoral character. The Supreme Court of Virginia is the only court to date that has passed on this question, concluding that the state's bar association could not block admittance on moral grounds to a woman because of her nonmarital cohabitation. The court said, "[W]hile her living arrangement may be unorthodox and unacceptable to some segments of society, this conduct bears no rational connection to her fitness to practice law."[50]

What can a single person do if denied a job or been otherwise discriminated against in employment because the person is single or living with someone to whom he is not married?

If the party is a private employer, you must check state law to determine whether you are covered by antidiscrimination provisions. The Appendix lists the states that have enacted such provisions. Moreover, each of these states has an executive agency with investigatory and in some instances enforcement power. If you live in one of those states it is imperative that you contact the proper agency as soon as possible as many of these laws require the filing of a complaint within a specific time frame. Failure to comply with these regulations may deprive you of your ability to seek redress.

If you do not live within one of the states identified in the Appendix, you will want to consider filing a complaint with the Equal Employment Opportunity Commission, which has the power to enforce Title VII of the 1964 Civil Rights Act. However, as discussed earlier, it only has the authority to investigate and remedy those cases involving sex discrimination. In other words, the complaint must allege that the employer's policy singles out women as opposed to men or vice versa. Should this be the case, you are again advised to contact your local EEOC office as soon as possible, as Title VII also has fairly strict time requirements.

As for discrimination arising out of a federal employment situation, complaints must first be lodged with your agency or department's Equal Employment Opportunity counselor who will try to resolve the complaint informally. If this fails, you should file a written complaint of discrimination with the agency. Ultimately in all of these instances, if you are dissatisfied with the administrative decision, you will need to seek redress in the courts.

As for discrimination that is barred by the Constitution (for example, irrational classifications and/or highly intrusive regulations promulgated by school boards, local police departments, and other branches of state government), one's only recourse is to put the matter in a federal or state court. In these latter instances, many branches of the American Civil Liberties Union may be willing to provide legal assistance.

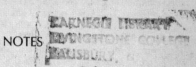

NOTES

1. Title VII of the Civil Rights Act of 1967, 42 U.S.C. §§2000e *et seq.*
2. 42 U.S.C. §2000e(b).
3. *Id.* at §2000e–2(b).
4. A limited form of protection is offered by the act to the extent that an employer's action against single women indicates sex discrimination. *See* notes 15–17 *infra.*
5. The particular language is taken from N.Y. EXEC. LAW §296(d).
6. *Manhattan Pizza Hut v. New York State Human Rights Appeal Board*, 415 N.E.2d 950, 953 (N.Y. 1980).
7. EEOC Decision Case No. 71–332 (1973), EEOC Dec. (CCH) ¶6164 (Sept. 8, 1970).
8. *Manhattan Pizza Hut, supra* note 6, at 953.
9. *Kraft v. State*, 284 N.W.2d 386 (Minn. 1979).
10. *Thompson v. Board of Trustees, School Dist. No. 12*, 627 P.2d 1229 (Mo. 1981).
11. *Washington Water Power Co. v. Washington State Human Rights Commission*, 586 P.2d 1149 (Wash. 1978).
12. *Klanseck v. Prudential Insurance Co.*, 509 F. Supp. 13 (E.D. Mich. 1980).
13. *Thompson v. Sanborn's Motor Express*, 382 A.2d 53 (N.J. Super. Ct. App. Div. 1977).
14. *Manhattan Pizza Hut, supra* note 6, at 950.
15. EEOC Decision Case No. 71–332 (1973), EEOC Dec. (CCH) ¶6164, p. 4276 (Sept. 8, 1970).
16. *Jacobs v. Martin Sweets Co.*, 550 F.2d 364, 370 (6th Cir. 1977).
17. *Grayson v. Wickes Corp.*, 607 F.2d 1194 (7th Cir. 1979).
18. *See* 29 U.S.C. §156(b)(1); 42 U.S.C. §2000e–2(c).
19. 29 U.S.C. §158(a)(3)(A) and (B).

20. *Id.* at (d).

21. *Vaca v. Sipes*, 386 U.S. 171 (1967).

22. *Id.* at 192–93.

23. 5 U.S.C. §2302(b)(1)(E).

24. *Andrews v. Drew Municipal Separate School Dist.*, 507 F.2d 611 (5th Cir. 1975).

25. *Id.* at 614.

26. *Hollenbaugh v. Carnegie Free Library*, 436 F. Supp. 1328 (W.D. Pa. 1977), *aff'd* 578 F.2d 1374 (3rd Cir.), *cert. denied*, 439 U.S. 1052 (1978).

27. *Hollenbaugh, supra* note 26, at 1333.

28. *Id.* at 1323.

29. *Loving v. Virginia*, 388 U.S. 1 (1967).

30. *Skinner v. Oklahoma ex rel. Williamson*, 316 U.S. 535 (1942).

31. *Eisenstadt v. Baird*, 405 U.S. 438 (1972).

32. *Roe v. Wade*, 410 U.S. 113 (1973).

33. *Prince v. Massachusetts*, 321 U.S. 158 (1944).

34. *Pierce v. Society of Sisters*, 268 U.S. 510 (1925).

35. *Moore v. City of East Cleveland*, 431 U.S. 494 (1977).

36. *Schuman v. City of Philadelphia*, 470 F. Supp. 449, 459 (E.D. Pa. 1979).

37. *Drake v. Covington County Board of Education*, 371 F. Supp. 974 (M.D. Ala. 1974) (a teacher's right of privacy was violated by a school board termination on grounds of pregnancy outside of marriage); *Schuman v. City of Philadelphia, supra* note 36 (a police officer's right of privacy was violated by his discharge); *Swope v. Bratton*, 541 F. Supp. 99 (W.D. Ark. 1982) (a police officer's private relations cannot be the basis of a discharge action); *Briggs v. North Muskegon Police Dep't.*, 563 F. Supp. 585 (W.D. Mich. 1983) (a police officer's dismissal violated both associational and privacy rights).

38. *Shawgo v. Spradlin*, 701 F.2d 470, 481 (5th Cir. 1983) (affirming a police department policy proscribing cohabitation of police officers); *Johnson v. San Jacinto Junior College*, 498 F. Supp. 555 (S.D. Tex. 1980) (a professor's adulterous relationship is not protected by the Constitution); *Brown v. Bathke*, 416 F. Supp. 1194 (D. Neb. 1976) (a school board interest in selecting staff who will impart social values outweighs a teacher's right of privacy).

39. *Hollenbaugh v. Carnegie Free Library, cert. denied*, 439 U.S. 1052 (1978); *Shawgo, supra* note 26, *cert. denied* 104 S.Ct. 404 (1983) (on both occasions Justice Marshall dissented from the denial stating that the right to privacy should have afforded the protection sought).

40. 5 U.S.C. §2302(b)(10).

41. 94 Stat. 2885 (1980)(repealing 10 U.S.C. §§3814 and 8814).

42. *Chappell v. Wallace*, 76 L. Ed. 2d 586, 593 (1983). ("This Court has never held, nor do we now hold, that military personnel are barred

from all redress in civil courts for constitutional wrongs suffered in the course of military service.")

43. *Id.* at 591 ("Civilian courts must, at the very least, hesitate long before entertaining a suit which asks the court to tamper with the established relationships between enlisted personnel and their superior officers.").

44. *Shawgo, supra* note 38, at 483.

45. Exec. Order No. 10,856, 25 Fed. Reg. 1583 (1960), *as amended*, 32 C.F.R. 155.4(a).

46. 32 C.F.R., at 155.4(e).

47. *Adams v. Laird*, 420 F.2d 230 (D.C. Cir. 1969), *cert. denied*, 397 U.S. 1039 (1970); *Gayer v. Schlesinger*, 490 F.2d 740 (D.C. Cir. 1973), *as amended*, 494 F.2d 1135 (1974).

48. *Schware v. Board of Bar Examiners*, 353 U.S. 232, 239 (1957).

49. *Id.*

50. *Cord v. Gibb*, 254 S.E.2d 71, 73 (Va. 1979).

V.

Personal Finances

Ownership of Property and Contracts Between Cohabitants

Can unmarried cohabitants own property jointly?

Yes. Cohabitants may own property as joint tenants with the right of survivorship. This means that each coowner has an undivided equal interest in the property, irrespective of how much each contributed. If one of the coowners dies, the property belongs entirely to the other coowner and does not pass through the deceased coowner's estate.

Cohabitants may also own property as tenants in common. Each tenant in common owns an agreed upon share of the property; the shares need not be equal. There is no right of survivorship in a tenancy in common. If one coowner dies, his or her share of the property passes into the estate and is distributed in accordance with the deceased's will or state intestacy laws. Intestacy laws apply when a person dies without a will.

When people who are not married acquire property jointly, the law presumes that they own it as tenants in common unless the document reflecting ownership states that they are joint owners. The precise language required to create a joint tenancy varies from state to state, but the safest language to use in any jurisdiction is as follows: "[the parties' names], as joint tenants with right of survivorship, and not as tenants in common."[1]

Can unmarried cohabitants own property as community property?

No. Community property—a system of ownership used in eight southern and western states—applies only to married couples.

Are cohabitants liable for the debts of each other?

Not unless the one who has not incurred the debt has undertaken to be responsible for its payment.

Do cohabitants have any legal obligation to support each other?

No laws require unmarried cohabitants to support each other. And no state awards alimony or other support payments when an unmarried couple separates. If, however, the cohabitants have entered a contract under which one agrees to support the other, the contract may be enforced (depending on the state in which the cohabitants live or the contract was established). Lawsuits brought to enforce these contracts have been popularly called *palimony* cases. But, since cohabitants seeking recovery under such an agreement are doing so on the basis of an express or implied contract and not on an alimony statute, the word *palimony* is actually inaccurate.

What happens to the property owned by cohabitants if they end their relationship?

Traditionally, unless a couple has an express written agreement to the contrary, the law has left matters as they are. Thus, when a couple separates, the property goes to whoever has legal title to it. Usually, this has meant that the man gets the property, because in relationships in which the man is the wage earner and the woman the homemaker, the wage earner "owns" the property acquired through his wages.[2]

In addition, until recently, most state courts refused to enforce even express agreements between cohabitants as to support or ownership of property. These courts have followed two main lines of reasoning. First, they have based their refusal on the grounds that such agreements are invalid because they are based on "illicit sexual services." For any contract to be valid, it must be based on something of value, or what the law calls consideration. Consideration cannot be illegal. The typical consideration in business contracts is money, services, property, or goods. Traditionally, courts have ignored the fact that most contracts between cohabitants are based on similar types of consideration. They have assumed either that the only services exchanged are sexual services or that, because sexual services form even part of the agreement, they invalidate the entire agreement.[3]

The second line of reasoning courts have used in refusing to enforce contracts between cohabitants is that homemaking services have no dollar value, so are not sufficient consideration to support an agreement to share property or to provide support.[4]

Some state courts still adhere to this traditional view. But since the California Supreme Court's 1976 decision in *Marvin v. Marvin*,[5] many state courts have upheld the contractual rights of cohabitants.

What did the *Marvin* decision hold?

The 1976 *Marvin* decision established four important legal principles. First, it held that courts should enforce express contracts between unmarried cohabitants except to the extent that a contract is founded explicitly on the consideration of "meritricious sexual services." An express contract is an explicit agreement between two parties. It can be oral or written. In reaching this conclusion, the court reasoned:

> [A]dults who voluntarily live together and engage in sexual relations are nonetheless as competent as any other persons to contract respecting their earnings and property rights. Of course, they cannot lawfully contract to pay for the performance of sexual services, for such a contract is, in essence, an agreement for prostitution and unlawful for that reason.[6]

Second, *Marvin* held that even if the parties have not entered an express contract, the courts should look at the conduct of the parties to determine if their conduct demonstrates an implied contract or some other tacit understanding between the parties (such as an agreement of partnership or joint venture). An implied contract is an agreement that is *inferred from the behavior* of the parties even though they have not made an explicit agreement. An implied contract is as valid as an express contract but it is more difficult to prove.

Third, *Marvin* held that even in the absence of an express or implied contract, courts may employ equitable remedies to prevent the unjust enrichment of one partner at the other's expense. The most commonly used equitable remedy is an award of the value of services rendered. In *Marvin*, the court said that it would be appropriate to award an unmarried cohabitant the reasonable value of household services rendered less the reasonable value of support received if (s)he can show that (s)he rendered the services with the expectation of monetary reward.[7]

Finally, *Marvin* established the principle that housekeeping services can provide adequate consideration for a contract to provide support or to share property.[8]

The California Supreme Court sent the *Marvin* case back to the lower court for a trial. (The case had never been tried because the trial court had dismissed it for failing to state valid grounds for relief.) At the trial, Michele Triola Marvin tried to prove that Lee Marvin had agreed to support her and that the two of them had agreed to pool their earnings and to share equally in all property acquired during their seven-year cohabitation. The trial court found that she did not prove that she and Lee Marvin had entered into either an express contract or an implied contract. It also ruled that she was not entitled to any equitable relief because Lee Marvin was not unjustly enriched at her expense. Nevertheless, the trial court did award Ms. Marvin $104,000 "for rehabilitation purposes."[9] This award, however, was disallowed by the appellate court.[10]

What is important about *Marvin v. Marvin* is not the actual result in that case, but the principles that the California Supreme Court established.

Is *Marvin v. Marvin* binding on other states?

No. Decisions by a state court are binding on only lower courts within that state. State courts, however, frequently look to decisions in other states when ruling on similar issues. Because *Marvin v. Marvin* was so widely publicized and dealt with such a topical issue, virtually every court considering claims by cohabitants has referred to the *Marvin* decision.

Several of these courts have rejected the principles established in *Marvin*. But many more have adopted its reasoning and holdings—in whole or in part.

What have other states held in cases similar to *Marvin*?

The following states have decided cases dealing with the contract and property rights of unmarried cohabitants. Unless otherwise indicated, the decisions summarized are of the states' highest courts and are, therefore, binding throughout the state. Decisions of lower courts are noted as such; these decisions are *not* binding throughout the state.

Alaska. The Alaska Supreme Court has ruled that both express and implied contracts between cohabitants are enforceable.[11] The court has expressly left open the question as to whether or not equitable relief is available.[12]

Connecticut. The Connecticut Superior Court (not the state's highest court) ruled that an agreement between cohabitants to combine income and to divide assets equally was enforceable. The court did not say whether the agreement was oral or implied, but it seemed to infer the contract from the parties' conduct. The court did not consider whether equitable relief was available.[13]

Florida. The Florida District Court of Appeals (not Florida's highest court) held that express contracts between cohabitants are enforceable as long as they are based on a consideration separate from any agreement about sexual relations. Although it did not rule on whether it would recognize implied contracts or grant equitable relief, the court suggested that it might allow recovery on those theories.[14]

Georgia. The Georgia Supreme Court held that contracts between cohabitants about support or ownership of property are unenforceable. The court also refused to award equitable relief.[15]

Hawaii. In Hawaii's only reported decision on this issue, the circuit court (not the state's highest court) held that when a man and woman have cohabited for many years, have had children and have held themselves out to the public as husband and wife, and when "the role of each person is duplicative of the roles of married male and female," a court may award one or the other cohabitant a portion of the property accumulated during the relationship.[16]

Illinois. The Illinois Supreme Court refused to enforce

even an express contract between a man and woman who had lived together for fifteen years, had three children and lived "a most conventional, respectable and ordinary family life." The court also ruled that cohabitants may not recover on theories of implied contract or unjust enrichment.[17]

Indiana. The Indiana Court of Appeals (not the highest court) ruled that a woman who cohabited with a man was entitled to a portion of jointly acquired property on theories of both express contract and implied contract. In addition, the court suggested that equitable relief might be available.[18]

Maryland. The Maryland Court of Special Appeals (not the highest court) enforced an express oral contract by which a man promised his lover to give her a thousand shares of bank stock in exchange for expenditures and services she provided for him. The two lovers were not cohabitants, but the man—who was married to someone else—maintained an apartment at which he regularly saw the woman.[19]

Massachusetts. In the only reported decision in this state since *Marvin*, the Massachusetts Supreme Judicial Court held that a woman who had cohabited with a man for less than a year was not entitled to *support* from him. Because the woman did not claim that she had entered into any kind of contract with her cohabiting partner, this case does not indicate what the Massachusetts high court's position is regarding contracts between cohabitants.[20]

Michigan. Michigan's Court of Appeals (not its highest court) has ruled that an express contract between cohabitants is enforceable.[21] It has also ruled that equitable relief is not available in suits between cohabitants.[22] Its rule on implied contracts seems to be that an implied contract will not be recognized between cohabitants when one cohabitant has rendered only domestic services, but that it may be found when the cohabitant has rendered services other than domestic services—for example, working in the other cohabitant's business.[23]

Minnesota. In Minnesota's only reported decision on this question, the Minnesota Supreme Court allowed recovery on purely equitable grounds. The cohabitants had lived together for twenty-one years, raised a son and held themselves out to the public as husband and wife. Although the man had supplied virtually all of the money for the property in question, and although some of the property was held in joint tenancy, the court awarded the woman half of all the property. The court did not discuss whether contracts between cohabitants are enforceable. But the court's apparent approval of *Marvin v. Marvin* and the generosity of its award suggest that it would enforce both express and implied contracts.[24]

Missouri. The Missouri courts have not dealt with contracts between cohabitants, but in a case dealing with related issues, the court of appeals (not Missouri's highest court) indicated that domestic services could constitute a contribution toward the acquisition of property.[25]

Nebraska. The Nebraska Supreme Court enforced an express oral contract by which one cohabitant promised the other to support her for the rest of her life if she would live with him and provide domestic services. Because the woman proved the existence of an express contract, the court did not discuss whether it would recognize an implied contract or provide equitable relief.[26]

New Hampshire. The New Hampshire Supreme Court has stated that it will enforce express contracts between cohabitants, but that it will not permit recovery for domestic services under an implied contract or an equitable theory. The court said, however, that it would permit recovery for services other than normal domestic services rendered between cohabitants.[27]

New Jersey. The New Jersey Supreme Court has ruled that both express and implied agreements between cohabitants are enforceable. The court has not ruled on whether equitable relief is available.[28]

New Mexico. In New Mexico's only reported decision on this question, the supreme court would not recognize an implied agreement between cohabitants to share property. The court did not discuss whether it would enforce an express agreement because the plaintiff did not prove one.[29]

New York. The New York Court of Appeals (the highest court) has ruled that express contracts between cohabitants are enforceable provided that sexual relations are not part of the consideration for the contract. It also ruled that New York courts will *not* imply a contract from the rendition of domestic services by cohabitants. The courts did not discuss whether equitable relief is available, but it would probably hold that it is not.[30]

Oregon. The Oregon Supreme Court has repeatedly held that both express and implied contracts between cohabitants are enforceable.[31] The court discussed in some detail the evidence from which it would infer an agreement to share,[32] and a number of lower courts in Oregon have found such agreements between cohabitants.

Pennsylvania. The Pennsylvania Superior Court (not the highest court) has held that express contracts between cohabitants are enforceable as long as the contract is supported by consideration other than sexual relations.[33] No reported Pennsylvania case has dealt with implied contracts or equitable relief.

Tennessee. A Tennessee chancery court (not the highest court) has said that cohabitants are not entitled to relief under theories of breach of express contract, breach of implied contract, or unjust enrichment.[34]

Washington. Although the Washington courts have repeatedly expressed dissatisfaction with the rule that property acquired by cohabitants belongs to the one in whose name legal title to the property stands, they have not overruled it. In several modern cases, the Supreme Court stated that it would reconsider the rule if the proper case came before it.[35]

Wisconsin. In a case brought by a woman against the estate of her deceased cohabitant, the Wisconsin Supreme Court held that the plaintiff was entitled to recover the value of services she performed for the deceased on the basis of implied contract. The court also suggested that such an award could be made on the theory of unjust enrichment.[36] Presumably, the court would also enforce express contracts.

Wyoming. The Wyoming Supreme Court held that an express oral contract between two cohabitants was enforceable as long as sexual services are not the consideration.[37] The court did not decide whether relief was available on the basis of implied contract or unjust enrichment.[38]

What reasons do courts give for refusing to recognize contracts between unmarried cohabitants?

The courts in three states—Georgia, Illinois, and Tennessee—refuse any relief to cohabitants seeking to recover for personal services. The only reason stated by the Georgia Supreme Court was that: "The parties being unmarried and the [woman] having admitted the fact of cohabitation..., this would constitute immoral consideration..."[39] This reasoning is entirely unpersuasive because, as the two judges who disagreed with the court's ruling pointed out, it had not been shown that sex was part of the consideration for the contract.[40]

The Illinois Supreme Court reasoned that recognizing contracts between cohabitants would violate the public policy reflected in the recently enacted Illinois Marriage and Dissolution of Marriage Act. That act reflected a "strong promarriage policy" and abolished common law marriage.[41]

The Tennessee Chancery Court reasoned: "A contract for an immoral purpose (living and cohabiting together without the benefit of marriage) is not only invalid consideration, but is for an immoral purpose and is contrary to public policy and will not be enforced."[42] It refused equitable relief because "'he who hath committed iniquity shall not have equity and no right of action arises out of an immoral transaction.'"[43]

Why do several courts enforce express contracts but not implied contracts?

The New York Court of Appeals's explanation for the difference is that "it is not reasonable to infer an agreement to pay for services rendered when the relationship of the parties makes it natural that the services were rendered gratuitously."[44] The court also expressed concern about fraudulent claims and a "substantially greater risk of emotion-laden afterthought" in trying to prove what the parties intended if there is no express agreement. Similar concerns had led the state legislature to abolish common law marriage. So, the court concluded, it was up to the legislature to determine whether implied contracts for personal services between cohabitants should be recognized.[45] Other courts that treat the two forms of contracts differently rely on similar reasoning.[46]

Do courts treat contracts between cohabitants for business services differently from contracts for domestic services?

Yes. Courts have been much more inclined to award relief on theories of implied contract or unjust enrichment to cohabitants who have rendered business or professional services for their cohabiting partners. The Michigan Court of Appeals, for instance, which does not recognize implied contracts for purely domestic services, awarded a cohabitant who had provided domestic *and* commercial services the value of her commercial services on theories of implied contract and unjust enrichment.[47] Similarly, the New Hampshire Supreme Court, which has held that cohabitants cannot recover for domestic services on the basis of implied contract or unjust enrichment, stated that "this holding is not meant to limit recovery for business and personal services, other than normal domestic services, rendered between unmarried cohabitants."[48]

Why do some courts distinguish between domestic and professional services?

There are several explanations for the distinction. First, many courts have presumed that domestic services are performed gratuitously.[49] They reason that in the normal course of life, persons living together in a close relationship perform services for each other without expecting payment.[50] This presumption is not applicable to professional services, for which the normal presumption is that if such services are performed and accepted, they are to be paid for.

Second, some courts consider household services to have no economic value. This, obviously, is not true of professional services. Finally, when the services are purely professional, there is no possibility that the contract rests on the consideration of illicit sexual services.

What sort of conduct has led courts to find implied contracts between cohabitants?

When courts look at the conduct of the parties to see if any agreement can be inferred from it, they focus on what the parties' intentions were with respect to ownership of property, compensation for services, or support in the future. It is difficult to generalize about what conduct reflects such intentions, but the following cases provide examples of evidence from which courts have implied agreements.

The Minnesota Supreme Court held that proof that the parties lived together for twenty-one years, raised a son, held themselves out to the public as husband and wife, and held their home and some personal property as joint tenants was sufficient to show that they intended that all their property would be divided equally.[51] The Oregon Supreme Court stated, "Cohabitation itself can be relevant evidence of an agreement to share incomes during continued cohabitation." It also said that "joint acts of a financial nature," such as joint checking accounts, joint savings accounts, and joint purchases, can give rise to an inference that the parties intended to share equally.[52] The Wisconsin Supreme Court affirmed a trial court's conclusion that a contract for services could be implied from the facts that the plaintiff performed housekeeping, farming, and nursing services at the instance and with the knowledge of her cohabitant and that the plaintiff expected compensation for these services.[53]

Have any of the courts that recognize contracts between cohabitants refused to enforce a contract because it was based on sexual services?

As just discussed, all of the courts that have held that contracts for personal services between cohabitants are enforceable, have stated or implied that the contracts must be supported by consideration independent of sexual relations.[54] In only one case, however, has a court refused to enforce a contract on the ground that there was no consideration independent of sexual relations.

In that case, two males entered into a "cohabitors agreement," by which they would hold themselves out as "cohabiting mates." One cohabitant would render his services to the other as a "lover, companion, homemaker, traveling companion, housekeeper and cook." In return, the other would provide financial support for the rest of the cohabitant's life, and they would share equally in all property accumulated during the relationship. A California court of appeals refused to enforce the agreement because the "plaintiff's rendition of sexual services to [his cohabitant] was an inseparable part of the consideration for the 'cohabitors agreement,' and indeed was the predominant consideration."[55] The court said that the terms *cohabiting* and *lover* could pertain only to the "rendition of sexual services," and it found no severable portion of the cohabitors' agreement supported by independent consideration.[56]

This decision does not seem compatible with the other decisions enforcing contracts between cohabitants. To be sure, the language in this contract was more explicit than that in most of the cases in which contracts between cohabitants have been enforced, but the substance of the contract was virtually identical. In most cohabitation contracts, the parties have implicitly agreed to be lovers, but the courts have found that that agreement did not invalidate whatever else the parties had agreed to in the contract. Although in this case the court did not indicate that the couple's sexual orientation had anything to do with the decision, the fact that the two parties were homosexual may have been what led the court to refuse to enforce their contract. The main lesson to be drawn from this case is that if you put your cohabitation agreement in writing, do not make any reference to the sexual aspects of your arrangement.

Has any court ever awarded temporary relief to a cohabitant suing for support?

Temporary relief—or relief during the pendency of a lawsuit—is frequently awarded in alimony cases. But, because the cases in which cohabitants seek support are generally for breach of contract, and thus not analogous to alimony cases, temporary relief is not awarded. In one recent decision, however, the New Jersey Supreme Court awarded an unmarried cohabitant $125 a week and the right to remain in the home during the pendency of her suit to enforce an agreement for support.[57] This decision is unusual and is unlikely to be widely followed.

How can two cohabitants make sure that their property is distributed as they wish in the event that their relationship ends?

The best way to insure that property is owned and will be distributed as the parties wish is to write up a contract defining the rights and obligations of both parties. Although a couple may want to consult a lawyer, it is not necessary that a lawyer draft the contract. Cohabitation agreements, unlike wills, need not meet legal formalities in order to be effective. A number of recent books discuss how to draft cohabitation agreements.

As just discussed, courts in a few states will not enforce even written agreements between cohabitants. In these states, a cohabitation agreement might still be helpful because the agreement would spell out the understanding of the parties and might be self-enforcing. In any state, the contract should not deal with the sexual aspects of the relationship.

NOTES

1. *See* O. Browder, R. Cunningham, and J. Julin, *Basic Property Law* 294–98 (2d ed. 1973).
2. L. Weitzman, *The Marriage Contract* 377 (1981).
3. *See id.* at 386–87.
4. *See, e.g., Keene v. Keene*, 371 P.2d 329 (Cal. 1962).
5. *Marvin v. Marvin*, 557 P.2d 106 (Cal. 1976).
6. *Id.* at 116.
7. *Id.* at 122–23.
8. *Id.* at 113 n.5.
9. 5 Fam. L. Rep. (BNA) 3077 (Cal. Super. Apr. 18, 1979).
10. 176 Cal. Rptr. 555 (Ct. App. 1981).
11. *Levar v. Elkins*, 604 P.2d 602 (Alaska 1980).
12. *Hill v. Ames*, 606 P.2d 388 (Alaska 1980).
13. *Dosek v. Dosek*, 4 Fam. L. Rep. (BNA) 2828 (Conn. Super. Ct. Oct. 4, 1978).
14. *Poe v. Estate of Levy*, 411 So. 2d 253 (Fla. Dist. Ct. App. 1982).
15. *Rehak v. Mathis*, 238 S.E.2d 81 (Ga. 1977).
16. *Artiss v. Artiss*, 8 Fam. L. Rep. (BNA) 2313 (Hawaii Cir. Ct. Jan. 5, 1982).
17. *Hewitt v. Hewitt*, 394 N.E.2d 1204 (Ill. 1979).
18. *Glasgo v. Glasgo*, 410 N.E.2d 1325 (Ind. Ct. App. 1980).
19. *Donovan v. Scuderi*, 443 A.2d 121 (Md. Ct. Spec. App. 1982).
20. *Davis v. Misiano*, 366 N.E.2d 752 (Mass. 1977).
21. *See Tyranski v. Piggins*, 205 N.W.2d 595 (Mich. Ct. App. 1973). *See also Carnes v. Sheldon*, 311 N.W.2d 747 (Mich. Ct. App. 1981).
22. *See Carnes, supra* note 21; *Roznowski v. Bozyk*, 251 N.W.2d 606 (Mich. Ct. App. 1977).
23. *See Carnes, supra* note 21; *Rosnowski, supra* note 22.
24. *Carlson v. Olson*, 256 N.W.2d 249 (Minn. 1977).
25. *Brooks v. Kunz*, 637 S.W.2d 135, 137 n.2 (Mo. Ct. App. 1982).
26. *Kinkenon v. Hue*, 301 N.W.2d 77 (Neb. 1981).
27. *Tapley v. Tapley*, 449 A.2d 1218 (N.H. 1982).
28. *Kozlowski v. Kozlowski*, 403 A.2d 902 (N.J. 1979).
29. *Merrill v. Davis*, 9 Fam. L. Rep. (BNA) 2718 (N.M. Sept. 14, 1983).
30. *Morone v. Morone*, 407 N.E.2d 438 (N.Y. 1980).
31. *See, e.g., Beal v. Beal*, 577 P.2d 507 (Or. 1978); *Latham v. Latham*, 547 P.2d 144 (Or. 1976).

32. *See Beal, supra* note 31.
33. *Baldassari v. Baldassari,* 420 A.2d 556 (Pa. Super. Ct. 1980).
34. *Roach v. Button,* 6 Fam. L. Rep. (BNA) 2355 (Tenn. Ch. Ct. Feb. 29, 1980).
35. *See Hinkle v. McColm,* 575 P.2d 711 (Wash. 1978); *Latham v. Hennessey,* 554 P.2d 1057 (Wash. 1976).
36. *In re Estate of Steffes,* 290 N.W.2d 697 (Wis. 1980).
37. *Kinnison v. Kinnison,* 627 P.2d 594 (Wyo. 1981).
38. *See id.* at 596.
39. *Rehak v. Matthis,* 238 S.E.2d 81, 82 (Ga. 1977).
40. *See id.* at 83.
41. *Hewitt, supra* note 17.
42. *Roach, supra* note 34.
43. *Id.* at 2356.
44. *Morone, supra* note 30, at 441.
45. *Id.* at 442.
46. *See Carnes, supra* note 23; *Tapley, supra* note 27.
47. *See Roznowski v. Bozyk, supra* note 22.
48. *Tapley, supra* note 27, at 1220.
49. *See, e.g., Williams v. Payne,* 515 S.W.2d 618 (Ky. Ct. App. 1974).
50. *See York v. Place,* 544 P.2d 572 (Or. 1975).
51. *Carlson, supra* note 24.
52. *Beal, supra* note 32.
53. *See In re Estate of Steffes, supra* note 36.
54. *See* discussion at pages 56–61.
55. *Jones v. Daly,* 176 Cal Rptr. 130, 133 (Ct. App. 1981).
56. *See id.*
57. *Crowe v. DeGioia,* 447 A.2d 173 (N.J. 1982).

Decedents' Estates

If two unmarried people are living together, and one dies without a will, can the other recover a portion of the estate under state inheritance laws?

No. All states have statutes providing for how a decedent's estate is to be distributed if (s)he dies without a will. Under these statutes, the estate passes to the deceased's spouse and children and, if there are none, to the parents or other blood relatives.[1] No state provides for a share of the estate to pass to the deceased's cohabiting partner.

Can a single person name his or her cohabiting partner as a beneficiary in his or her will?

Yes. An individual can name anyone (s)he wishes as a beneficiary in a will. In fact, the best way for a person to insure that all or part of an estate passes to the cohabiting partner is to so provide in a properly executed will. The rules for properly executing a will vary from state to state. It is essential that these rules be followed scrupulously in order to insure that the will survives a legal challenge. Although the law does not require that a will be prepared by a lawyer, you should consult one if your estate is large or if you wish to make a complex distribution. You should also consult a lawyer if you are at all uncertain about any of the requirements of a properly executed will.

Can a single person name his or her cohabiting partner as a beneficiary of a life insurance policy?

Yes. One can name anyone the beneficiary of a life insurance policy, and the majority rule is that a named beneficiary may collect the insurance proceeds despite his or her cohabitation with the insured.[2]

A few cases, however, have held that a cohabitant who was the named beneficiary could not collect the proceeds of the policy because she was improperly described by the insured as his wife.[3] The courts reasoned that the false representation was material and that the insurance company would not have issued the policy if it knew that the insured was cohabiting with the beneficiary. These cases, however, are in a clear minority. In nearly all of the cases in which the named beneficiary had been falsely described as *wife*, the courts held that the term was merely descriptive and did not affect the beneficiary's right to collect.[4] Nevertheless, it makes much more sense to avoid any such problem by properly describing the cohabitant, if a description is required.

Can a single person take out insurance on the life of his or her cohabiting partner?

There may be problems with this. In order to purchase life insurance, a person must have an *insurable interest* in the life of the person to be insured.[5] The policy behind this rule is to avoid inducement for homicide and to prevent wagering contracts.[6] The definition of *insurable interest* found in New York's insurance law, which is typical, is: (a) the interest of close relatives; or (b) a substantial economic interest in having the life of the insured continue.[7]

Although a cohabitant may fit this statutory definition, it is conceivable that an insurance company or a court would determine that a cohabitant has no insurable interest in his or her cohabiting partner.[8] To avoid this possibility, the person to be insured should take out the policy and name his or her cohabitant as beneficiary of the policy. (This option does have different tax consequences and, as with writing a will, if a large estate is involved, an attorney should be consulted.)

Can a cohabitant recover part of his or her deceased cohabitant's estate on the theory that the deceased had promised to share property accumulated during the relationship or to pay for domestic or other services?

It depends on the state. The law in this area closely parallels the law applicable when two cohabitants end their relationship (see pages 55–56). Thus, in states that recognize contracts between cohabitants, if the surviving cohabitant can prove that the two cohabitants had entered into a contract under which the deceased promised to pay the surviving cohabitant or to share ownership of certain (or all) property accumulated during the relationship, that contract will probably be enforced. In states that do not recognize such contracts, the surviving cohabitant most likely cannot recover anything on this theory.

How can the surviving cohabitant prove that (s)he had such a contract with the deceased?

If the surviving cohabitant has a written contract that the deceased would share ownership or pay for services or something similar, (s)he would probably have little difficulty enforcing this contract.

If there is no written contract, however, the surviving cohabitant will have much more trouble. The surviving partner must prove that he and the deceased had made an oral contract or that a contract can be implied from the actions of the two. (An oral contract is an explicit *oral* agreement between two parties. An implied contract is an agreement that is *inferred from the behavior* of the parties even though they may not have formulated an explicit agreement.)[9]

Generally, an oral contract or an implied contract is just as valid as a written contract. Nevertheless, a few courts have refused to imply contracts between cohabitants even though they do enforce express contracts (see page 62). In addition, it is much more difficult to prove an oral contract or an implied contract than a written contract.

What problems would the surviving cohabitant face in trying to prove an oral contract?

The major difficulty would be convincing the judge or jury that the deceased had promised to share all or some property or to pay for his or her services (or whatever the alleged promise is). Because the promisor is dead and the survivor obviously has a strong interest in the matter, the surviving cohabitant's testimony may not be believed.

In addition, most states have evidentiary rules that make it difficult, if not impossible, to prove that the deceased made such a promise. Most states have "dead man's laws," which prevent a claimant against an estate from testifying about transactions or communications with the deceased.[10] (The "logic" behind these laws is to protect decedents' estates from plundering by perjurers.) Other states require the survivor's testimony to be buttressed by other evidence, most commonly testimony by a disinterested person.[11] Since most conversations creating a contract about such personal matters would not have taken place in the presence of third persons, these evidentiary rules often make it impossible to prove an oral contract with a deceased cohabitant.[12]

Finally, many states require a person making a claim against an estate to prove the claim by "clear and convincing evidence."[13] This standard of proof is substantially more difficult to satisfy than the "preponderance of the evidence" standard applied in most noncriminal cases.

While these obstacles may be difficult, they are not insurmountable. Cohabitants have recovered under such contracts.[14]

What problems would the surviving cohabitant have in trying to prove an implied contract?

The most likely implied contract a surviving cohabitant would try to prove is a contract to pay for housekeeping, business, or other services. To prove an implied contract for services, a claimant must show: (1) that the services were rendered at the request of the deceased, (2) that the claimant expected payment, and (3) that the deceased intended to compensate the claimant.[15]

A cohabitant seeking to prove an implied contract for services will have a difficult time making such a showing. In addition to the evidentiary problems discussed in proving an oral contract, the surviving cohabitant will probably have to overcome the legal presumption that when there is a close familial relationship, services are performed gratuitously. The theory underlying this presumption is that in the normal course of life, persons living together in a close relationship perform services for each other without expecting payment; they perform the services out of a feeling of affection or sense of obligation.[16] Several courts have applied this presumption to unmarried cohabitants.[17]

Again, despite these obstacles, courts have found implied contracts for services between cohabitants. The Wisconsin Supreme Court, for example, recently affirmed a lower court's award of $14,600 to a woman for two years of housekeeping, farming, and nursing services she performed for the man with whom she lived.[18] The court found that a contract to pay for her services could be implied because the services were performed at the instance, and with the knowledge of the deceased, the woman expected compensation for her services, and the deceased expressed his intent to provide for her. Although her opponent raised the presumption of gratuitous services, the court held that because a promise to pay could be implied from the facts of the case, the claimant was entitled to compensation regardless of the fact that she rendered the services with a sense of affection, devotion, and duty. The court found it unnecessary to decide whether the presumption of gratuitous services applied to unmarried cohabitants.[19]

Might a court find a contract to pay for services rendered or to share property to be void because the parties are involved in an "illicit" relationship?

It depends on the state. The states that refuse to enforce such contracts between two living cohabitants on this basis will doubtless refuse to enforce them against the estates of deceased cohabitants (see pages 58–61). Most of the courts that have been asked to enforce such contracts against a deceased's estate, however, have held that a contract between two people is not void merely because there is an "illicit" relationship, so long as the contract is not based on the performance of sexual services.[20] Other cases have gone so far as to say that contracts between cohabitants are void only when the contract rests only, or primarily, on the performance of sexual services.[21]

Are there other ways in which a cohabitant can recover part of the estate of his or her cohabitant?

Cohabitants may hold property as joint tenants or owners. Joint tenants have rights of survivorship. This means that property owned jointly would pass to the other cohabitant if one of them died.

In addition, in several cases, courts have awarded a surviving cohabitant the value of services rendered to the deceased, presumably on the theory that such an award was necessary to prevent injustice. Typically, the surviving cohabitant had tried to prove an oral or implied contract but, because of the restrictive evidentiary rules, failed.[22] Such an award lies entirely in the court's discretion and is not always made when the survivor has failed to prove a contract. Whether a claimant will be awarded the value of services rendered depends on both how sympathetic the facts of the case are and how tolerant the court is regarding claims by cohabitants.[23]

NOTES

1. *See, e.g.,* §§2–102–103 of the Uniform Probate Code (UPC). The UPC is a model code that has served as the pattern for 21 states and is closely followed by many others.
2. Alexander, "Meritricious Relationships with Respect to Life Insurance," 44 *Insurance Counsel J.* 321 (1977).
3. *See, e.g., Chitwood v. Prudential Insurance Co.,* 143 S.E.2d 915 (Va. 1965); *Continental Casualty Co. v. Lindsay,* 69 S.E. 344 (Va. 1910).
4. Alexander, "Life Insurance," *supra* note 2, at 325.

5. J. Appleman, *Insurance Law & Practice* §761 (1966).
6. *See id.*
7. N.Y. Ins. Law §146(2).
8. *See* L. Weitzman, *The Marriage Contract* 371 (1981).
9. *Id.* at 401.
10. *See McCormick on Evidence* §65 (2d ed. 1972).
11. *See, e.g.,* OR. REV. STAT. §115.195.
12. *See, e.g., Lawrence v. Ladd,* 570 P.2d 638 (Or. 1977). *See also McCormick on Evidence, supra* note 10.
13. *See, e.g., Gosch v. Estate of Gomez,* 450 P.2d 1016 (Colo. 1969); *In re Estate of Pomeroy,* 316 N.E.2d 231 (Ill. App. Ct. 1974); *Estate of Countryman,* 494 P.2d 1163 (Kan. 1972); *Estate of Allen,* 412 A.2d 833 (Pa. 1980).
14. *See, e.g., Tyranski v. Piggins,* 205 N.W.2d 595 (Mich. Ct. App. 1973).
15. *See In re Estate of Steffes,* 290 N.W.2d 697 (Wis. 1980).
16. *York v. Place,* 544 P.2d 572 (Or. 1975).
17. *See, e.g., Williams v. Payne,* 515 S.W.2d 618 (Ky. Ct. App. 1974); *York, supra* note 16.
18. *In re Estate of Steffes, supra* note 15.
19. *Id.* at 703–4.
20. *See, e.g., Tyranski, supra* note 14; *In re Estate of Steffes, supra* note 15.
21. *See Poe v. Estate of Levy,* 411 So.2d 253 (Fla. Dist. Ct. App. 1982); *Latham v. Latham,* 547 P.2d 144 (Or. 1976).
22. *See Humiston v. Bushnell,* 394 A.2d 844 (N.H. 1978); *Green v. Richmond,* 337 N.E.2d 691 (Mass. 1975). *See also In re Estate of Steffes, supra* note 15.
23. For a thorough treatment of remedies available to a cohabitant when his or her cohabiting partner dies, see Pfaff, "Death Is Not the Great Equalizer: Division of Marital Property," 14 *U.S.F. L. Rev.* 157 (1980).

Tax

Do two single people who live together and who are both employed pay more federal income tax than a similarly situated married couple?

Not unless there is a considerable disparity in income between the two cohabitants.

Generally, such cohabitants pay less income tax than a married couple in which both spouses work. In 1982, the federal tax law reduced this "marriage penalty" by allowing a special deduction for a married couple when both partners work. Even with this deduction, two-earner married couples usually pay greater taxes than unmarried couples. A married couple, for example, in which one spouse has an income of $40,000, and the other an income of $20,000, pays a joint income tax of $16,385 (assuming they do not itemize deductions). If this couple were not married and had to file separate returns, their income tax would be $14,429 ($10,979 and $3,450).

Two single people who live together pay more tax than a married couple, however, when there is a great disparity in the income of the two partners. An unmarried couple, for example, in which one partner has an income of $100,000 and the other $10,000, pays a total of $41,866 in separate income taxes ($40,818 and $1,048). If this same couple were married, they would pay a joint income tax of $41,199 (again, assuming they do not itemize deductions).

In addition to using different tax rates for single and married people, federal tax law treats deductions allowed to each group differently. An unmarried couple has an advantage in many of the deductions, such as the medical expense deduction, earned income credit, and investment credit. A married couple has an advantage in several other deductions, such as the political contributions deduction and exclusion from dividend income.

Does an unmarried couple in which only one partner has an income pay more federal income tax than a married couple in which only one spouse has an income?

Yes. The major advantage the federal income tax law affords to married couples—income splitting—is not available to unmarried couples. Income splitting attributes half of the married couple's income to each spouse and, under the progressive tax table, results in a lower tax than if all the income were attributed to one spouse. A married couple in which one partner has an income of $40,000 and the other has no income, pays $8,425 in income tax on a joint return (assuming they do not itemize deductions). A single person who has one unrelated dependent and who earns $40,000 pays $10,539.

Can an unmarried couple file a joint return?
No. Only married couples can file joint returns.

Can a single person with a dependent file an income tax return as "head of household" and thus be taxed at a lower rate?
Only if the dependent is a close relative of the taxpayer (by blood, marriage, or adoption). A single person is eligible for head of household status if the person paid more than half the cost of a home in which the dependent relative lives. A single person who provides a home for a dependent who is not a relative does not qualify for "head of household" status.[1]

If two unrelated people are living together, and only one works, can the working partner claim a dependency exemption for the nonworking partner?
Yes, if the nonworking partner (a) has less than a $1,000 income; (b) receives more than half of his or her support from the working partner; and (c) lives as a member of the working partner's household for the whole tax year.[2]

The exemption may *not* be taken, however, if the relationship violates any local law. A federal court of appeals held that a taxpayer was not allowed to take a dependency deduction for the woman he lived with because a North Carolina statute made it a misdemeanor for a man and woman to cohabit.[3]

The exemption may also be unavailable if the cohabitants have a *Marvin*-type agreement, under which one performs domestic services in exchange for food, shelter, and other living needs. In one case, the United States Tax Court held that a taxpayer with such an agreement could not take his cohabitant as a dependency deduction because the woman had received compensation for services rendered rather than support.[4]

Can a single person take the deduction for child care?
Yes. Marital and tax filing status are irrelevant in determining eligibility for the child care and dependent care deduction. If the taxpayer meets the requirements for the deduction, it makes no difference that he or she is single.[5]

Do unmarried persons suffer any disadvantage under federal estate and gift tax laws?

Yes. Both the estate tax marital deduction and the gift tax marital deduction—which provide significant tax savings to married couples—are unavailable to unmarried cohabitants.

Another gift tax advantage to married couples is the Internal Revenue Code's provision that a gift of one spouse is considered a gift of the other. Under the code, a person may make a gift of up to $10,000 in any one year without having to pay gift tax.[6] The code also provides that a spouse may allow half of any gift made by the other spouse to be deemed a gift of the consenting spouse.[7] Thus, a wife may give $20,000, and if her husband consents, each will be deemed to have made a gift of $10,000, and neither will have to pay a gift tax. This advantage is not available to unmarried couples.

NOTES

1. For precise requirements for filing as "head of household," *see* General Instructions to Income Tax Form 1040.
2. For more precise requirements, *see* Internal Revenue Service Publication 501.
3. *Ensminger v. Commissioner,* 610 F.2d 189 (4th Cir. 1979).
4. *Angstadt v. Commissioner,* 27 T.C.M. (CCH) 693 (1968).
5. For precise requirements for the child and dependent care deduction, *see* Internal Revenue Service Form 2441.
6. 26 U.S.C.A. §2503(b).
7. *Id.* at §2513.

Credit

Can a bank or other lender refuse to extend a mortgage or other credit to a single person because he or she is single or cohabiting with someone?

No. The federal Equal Credit Opportunity Act (ECOA) prohibits any creditor from discriminating against anyone on the basis of marital status in extending credit.[1] Many state laws have a similar prohibition.[2]

Can a bank or other lender discriminate between married and single people in establishing an interest rate?

No. The Equal Credit Opportunity Act prohibits this form of discrimination as well.

Can a lender refuse to combine the income of two unmarried people in determining their eligibility for a joint mortgage?

No. The Equal Credit Opportunity Act requires a creditor to treat an unmarried couple applying for credit jointly the same as it would treat them if they were married.[3]

Can a lender ask a credit applicant what his or her marital status is?

In some situations, yes. The Equal Credit Opportunity Act permits a lender to ask a credit applicant his or her marital status if it is necessary to ascertain the applicant's financial situation—for example, to find out whether the applicant is obligated to support someone else.[4] The ECOA also permits a lender to ask an applicant to designate a title (Mr., Ms., Mrs., or Miss) on an application form, but the form must indicate that designating a title is optional.[5] In addition, the regulations promulgated under the ECOA provide that lenders should ask applicants for mortgages on residential property what their marital status is. The purpose of the inquiry is to monitor whether lenders are complying with the ECOA and not discriminating on the basis of marital status. Again, however, the lender may not *require* applicants to disclose their marital status.[6] The ECOA makes it crystal clear that this information may not be used to discriminate against applicants on the basis of marital status.[7]

NOTES

1. 15 U.S.C.A. §1691.
2. *See, e.g.,* Ark. Stat. Ann. §70–925–929; N.J. Stat. Ann. §10:5–12(i).
3. *Markham v. Colonial Mortgage Service Co.,* 605 F.2d 566 (D.C. Cir. 1979).
4. 12 C.F.R. §202.6(b).

5. *Id.* at §202.5(d)(3).
6. *Id.* at §202.13.
7. 15 U.S.C.A. §1691.

Alimony

Are there laws that require termination of alimony if the alimony recipient cohabits with another person?

Yes. A number of states have statutes that provide for modification or termination of alimony if the alimony recipient cohabits with another person.

Statutes in Alabama, Illinois, Louisiana, Pennsylvania, and Utah provide that alimony is automatically terminated upon cohabitation.[1] The courts in these states, however, have discretion in deciding whether the alimony recipient is cohabiting according to the statutory language.

Six other states provide that courts *may* modify or terminate alimony upon cohabitation. In California, Connecticut, Oklahoma, and Tennessee, alimony may be modified or terminated only if the cohabitation has resulted in a decreased need for support by the alimony recipient.[2] The statutes of Georgia and New York leave it to the courts to decide whether alimony should be modified, but do not require that the cohabitation cause a change in the alimony recipient's financial situation.[3]

Do these statutes mandate that the cohabiting parties be engaged in sexual relations?

Five of the statutes expressly provide that the cohabitants be engaged in sexual relations.[4] Most of the courts that have faced the issue under the other statutes found there was no cohabitation in the absence of some sexual relations between the cohabitants.[5]

All but four of these statutes specify that the cohabiting partner be of the opposite sex.[6] Presumably, then, homosexual cohabitation under these statutes would not be grounds for terminating or modifying alimony.

Can alimony be modified because of cohabitation in states that do not have statutes specifically addressing the question?

Yes. First of all, many agreements incorporated into divorce decrees expressly provide that alimony will terminate upon cohabitation. Such provisions are enforceable.

Even without such an agreement or a statute, alimony may be modified if the cohabitation changes the alimony recipient's need for support. In most states, an alimony award may be modified if the financial situation of the alimony recipient changes substantially.[7] In these states, courts consider whether the cohabitation has reduced the financial needs of the alimony recipient. Cohabitation alone will not terminate alimony.[8]

NOTES

1. ALA. CODE §30–2–55; ILL. ANNOT. STAT. ch. 40 §510; LA. CIVIL CODE ANN. art. 160; PA. STAT. ANN. tit. 23 §507; UTAH CODE ANN. §30–3–5(3).
2. CALIF. CIV. CODE §4801.5; CONN. GEN. STAT. ANN. §46b-86; OKLA. STAT. tit. 12 §1289(D); TENN. CODE ANN. §36–820(a)(3).
3. GA. CODE §19–6–19(b); N.Y. DOM. REL. LAW §248.
4. GA. CODE §19–6–19(b); ILL. ANNOT. STAT. ch. 40 §510; LA. CIVIL CODE ANN. art. 160; OKLA. STAT. tit. 12 §1289(D); UTAH CODE ANN. §30–3–5(3).
5. *See, e.g., Hicks v. Hicks*, 405 So.2d 31 (Ala. Civ. App. 1981); *In re Marriage of Thweatt*, 157 Cal. Rptr. 826 (Ct. App. 1979).
6. The 4 states that do not specify that the cohabitants be of the opposite sex are Connecticut, Illinois, Louisiana, and Tennessee.
7. *See* Oldham, "Cohabitation by an Alimony Recipient Revisited," 20 J. Fam. L. 615, 620 (1981–82).
8. *See, e.g., Abbott v. Abbott*, 282 N.W.2d 561 (Minn. 1979); *Gayet v. Gayet*, 456 A.2d 102 (N.J. 1983); *Brister v. Brister*, 595 P.2d 1167 (N.M. 1979); *Myhre v. Myhre*, 296 N.W.2d 905 (S.D. 1980); *Van Gorder v. Van Gorder*, 327 N.W.2d 674 (Wis. 1983).

Government Benefits

Are there government benefits that are available to married people but are denied to single people who are cohabiting?

Yes. Unmarried cohabitants are not eligible for any of the Social Security benefits for old age, survivors, disability, or death that typically accrue to spouses. In addition, unrelated cohabitants cannot receive veterans and unemployment benefits available to related dependents.[1]

Can a woman who has a child with a man she cohabited with collect Social Security surviving mother's benefits when the man dies?

No. Surviving mother's benefits are available only to a deceased's lawful spouse and divorced spouse.[2] The United States Supreme Court has ruled that it is not unconstitutional to deny Social Security mother's insurance benefits to a woman who cohabited with a man and who bore his child.[3] The children, however, are entitled to survivors' benefits.[4]

Is AFDC available to single people?

Yes. A single parent who has custody of his or her child may receive Aid to Families with Dependent Children (AFDC) if the family otherwise meets state eligibility requirements.[5]

Can a family be denied AFDC because the parent is cohabiting with another person?

No. Fifteen years ago, the United States Supreme Court invalidated a state's "substitute father" regulation, under which AFDC payments were denied to the children of a mother who merely cohabited with an "able-bodied man" who had no legal duty to support her children.[6] The federal regulations now provide that if an unmarried cohabitant does not have a legal obligation to support the children or the mother, his income may not be assumed to be available to the family.[7] If, however, the cohabitant is actually contributing financially to the household, his support may be considered in determining the family's need for assistance.

Can a state require an unrelated person who lives with a family receiving AFDC to make a financial contribution to the family?

Yes. Some states require cohabitants to contribute to the support of the household. California, for example, requires an unrelated adult male, who lives with a family that receives aid, to make a financial contribution of at least as much as it would cost him to provide himself with an independent living arrangement.[8] This requirement has been challenged with varying results. In one case, a California appellate court upheld the constitutionality of the statute.[9] But in another case, a different California appellate court held that a state may not reduce aid on the basis of an *assumed* availability of income from an unrelated adult male residing in a household receiving AFDC, and that there must be proof of actual contribution.[10]

Can a family lose AFDC if the mother marries?

Perhaps. Under a recently enacted amendment to the AFDC laws, the income of a stepparent living in the household is included in the computation to determine eligibility for aid, even if the stepparent otherwise has no obligation to support the children.[11] Previously, pursuant to the Supreme Court's decision in *Lewis v. Martin*,[12] it could not be assumed that the income of a stepparent would be accessible to a child unless the state made the stepparent legally responsible as a natural or adoptive parent. Thus, if the stepfather has an income that exceeds AFDC eligibility requirements, the family will lose its aid.

Are single persons eligible for food stamps?

Yes, if the single person meets the income standards for participation in the food stamp program. Marital status is irrelevant in determining food stamp eligibility. The federal Food Stamp Act provides that food stamps are available to needy "households."[13] A *household* is defined as (a) an individual who lives alone; (b) an individual who lives with others, but who buys and prepares food separately from the others; or (c) a group of individuals who live together and customarily purchase food and prepare meals together.[14]

Are single persons who cohabit eligible for food stamps?

Yes, if their combined income satisfies the need requirements. As just discussed, food stamp eligibility is determined on the basis of "households." In *U.S. v. Moreno*,[15] the United States Supreme Court held that it was unconstitutional to exclude from the food stamp program any household containing an individual unrelated to any other member of the household.

Can an individual who would be eligible for food stamps if he or she lived alone, but who lives with someone who is not eligible, receive food stamps?

If the two people live and eat together, they will be treated as one household, and if their combined income exceeds the standard of eligibility for food stamps, the otherwise eligible individual cannot receive them.[16] If, however, the two individuals live together but do not buy and prepare food together, they are considered two households, and the individual may receive food stamps.[17] Similarly, two families who live together to save on rent are not considered a household for food stamp purposes if they have meals separately.[18]

NOTES

1. L. Weitzman, *The Marriage Contract* 368–69 (1981).
2. 42 U.S.C.A. §402(g).
3. *Califano v. Boles*, 443 U.S. 282 (1979).
4. *See also Chambers v. Harris*, 687 F.2d 332 (10th Cir. 1982).
5. AFDC is administered by the individual states, which establish their own eligibility requirements. However, in order for states to qualify for matching federal funds—which all the states do—the states must meet the standards of the federal AFDC statute. 42 U.S.C.A. §§601 *et seq*.
6. *King v. Smith*, 392 U.S. 309 (1968).
7. 45 C.F.R. §233.90(a)(1).
8. CAL. WELF. & INST. CODE §11351.5.
9. *Russell v. Carleson*, 111 Cal. Rptr. 497 (Cal. 3d Dist. Ct. App. 1973).
10. *North Coast Coalition v. Woods*, 168 Cal. Rptr. 95 (Cal. 1st Dist. Ct. App. 1980).
11. 42 U.S.C.A. §602(a)(3).
12. 397 U.S. 552 (1970).

13. 7 U.S.C.A. §§2011 *et seq.*
14. 7 C.F.R. §273.1(a).
15. 413 U.S. 528 (1973).
16. *See, e.g., Fife v. Blum,* 442 N.Y.S.2d 231 (N.Y. App. Div. 1981).
17. *See, e.g., Lasoff v. Blum,* 448 N.Y.S.2d 852 (N.Y. App. Div. 1982).
18. 7 C.F.R. §273.1(b)(7).

VI.
Child Bearing and Child Rearing

Abortion

Can a woman be denied an abortion because she is single?

No. The United States Supreme Court ruled in 1973, in *Roe v. Wade*, that a woman has a fundamental right, grounded in the constitutionally protected right of privacy, to have an abortion.[1] The case was brought by a single woman who challenged a Texas statute that severely restricted the right to have an abortion. In *Roe* the Court held that in order to restrict a woman's right to abortion, a state must have a "compelling interest."[2] The Court said that protection of the woman's health, maintenance of medical standards, and protection of prenatal life are important state interests that may supersede a woman's right to an abortion but only *after* the first three months of pregnancy.[3] During the first three months the decision of the woman and her doctor cannot be interfered with.[4]

What restrictions exist on the right to have an abortion since *Roe v. Wade*?

Since 1973, the Supreme Court has reviewed various restrictions that states and localities have placed on the right to abortion. The Court has held, for example, that a state may require the informed consent of the woman because the decision to abort is

> often a stressful one, and it is desirable and imperative that it be made with full knowledge of its nature and consequences. A woman is the one primarily concerned, and her awareness of the decision and its significance may be assured, constitutionally, by the State to the extent of requiring her prior written consent.[5]

Most recently, the Supreme Court reaffirmed its holding in *Roe v. Wade* and invalidated an Akron, Ohio ordinance that restricted the abortion right.[6] The Court held that a state cannot require a woman to have an abortion in a hospital after the first three months.[7] The Court also invalidated sections of the Akron ordinance that required certain information about the operation and the fetus to be told to a woman before she could have an abortion,[8] and that would force the woman to wait twenty-four hours after giving her written consent before an abortion could be performed.[9]

Can the consent of the unwed father be required before a woman can have an abortion?

Almost surely not. Although the Supreme Court has not directly addressed the question of whether an unwed father has any rights in a woman's decision to abort, it has held that a state may not require the consent of the spouse before a woman can abort.[10] The Court explained that "[i]nasmuch as it is the woman who physically bears the child and who is more directly and immediately affected by the pregnancy [than the husband], the balance weighs in her favor."[11] If the lawful husband cannot unilaterally "prohibit the wife from terminating her pregnancy,"[12] it would seem extremely unlikely that the Court would grant such right to an unwed father. The issue was directly addressed by a Florida appellate court after the Supreme Court's decision in *Roe v. Wade*.[13] Based on its analysis of *Roe*, the Florida court held that the unwed father had no right to prevent the natural mother from terminating the pregnancy.[14]

Must the unwed father be notified before a woman can have an abortion?

The Supreme Court has not ruled on this question. Some state statutes provide that the husband be notified before a woman can abort.[15] In a case involving the Illinois law, a federal court granted a preliminary injunction preventing enforcement of several sections of the act, one of which required spousal consultation.[16] A Florida statute requiring that the husband be notified of the proposed abortion also states that the notification provision does not apply if the "husband is voluntarily living apart or estranged."[17] If an estranged husband has no right of notification, it would seem that the unwed father equally would have no such rights. In a case involving restrictions on a minor's right to have an abortion, the Supreme Court upheld a parental notification provision for an immature, unemancipated minor who lived with, and was dependent on, her parents.[18] Although the Court upheld the notification requirement, the circumstances in the case were sufficiently narrow so that it seems unlikely that the Court would uphold as constitutional such a notification burden on an adult woman's right to have an abortion.

Can an unmarried minor be required to obtain the consent of her parents in order to have an abortion?

Sometimes. The Supreme Court has over the years recognized that states may restrict the freedom of children in certain ways that would be unconstitutional if applied to adults. "These rulings have been grounded in the recognition that, during the formative years of childhood and adolescence, minors often lack the experience, perspective, and judgment to recognize and avoid choices that could be detrimental to them."[19] Nonetheless, in 1976, the Supreme Court held that a state may not impose an *absolute* requirement of parental or guardian consent before an unmarried minor could obtain an abortion.[20]

Three years later, in *Bellotti v. Baird*, the Court evaluated a Massachusetts abortion statute that required parental or judicial consent before a minor could have an abortion.[21] The Court noted that the abortion decision is different from other decisions minors have to make in that denying a young woman the right to have an abortion will have, in the Court's words, "grave and indelible" consequences.[22] The Court found the statute unconstitutional because, although parental or judicial consent can constitutionally be required, a statute must provide for an alternative procedure for a mature minor to make her own decision, or if she is immature, for a finding that an abortion might nonetheless be in her best interests without parental consent.[23] This was an opinion joined by only four of the nine justices. Finally, in the 1983 case challenging the Akron ordinance just discussed, a full majority of the Court held that there cannot be "a blanket determination that *all* minors under the age of 15 are too immature to make this decision or that an abortion never may be in the minor's best interests without parental approval."[24] In other words, a statute must provide a procedure whereby each case can be analyzed and evaluated to determine the maturity and best interests of the minor.[25] At the same time it reviewed the Akron ordinance, the Supreme Court upheld a Missouri statute's requirement of a "consent substitute, either parental or judicial," before an immature minor can obtain an abortion.[26]

The rule, therefore, seems to be that a statute will withstand constitutional challenge if it (1) permits an unmarried minor to establish that she is mature enough to make the decision with her doctor; (2) provides for review by judicial approval; or (3) permits proof that an abortion without parental consent would nonetheless be in her best interests.

Can an unmarried minor be required to notify her parents before an abortion?

In some circumstances a state may require that an unmarried minor's parents be notified before she can have an abortion. This is *not* a parental consent requirement. In the first Supreme Court case addressing the issue of parental notification, a Utah statute required a doctor to notify, if possible, the parents or guardian of an unmarried minor before performing an abortion.[27] The Court held that the Utah notification requirement was valid as applied to a minor who lives with, and is dependent upon, her parents, is not emancipated, and has made no claim or showing as to her maturity.[28] A notification requirement is likely to become as great a barrier to a minor's right of choice as a consent requirement if many young women will forego consulting a doctor at all about an abortion if they know their parents will be notified.

NOTES

1. *Roe v. Wade*, 410 U.S. 113 (1973).
2. *Id.* at 155.
3. *Id.*
4. *Id.* at 163. For a more detailed discussion *see* the ACLU Handbook, *The Rights of Women*, by S. Deller Ross and A. Barcher (1983).
5. *Planned Parenthood v. Danforth*, 428 U.S. 52, 67 (1976).
6. *City of Akron v. Akron Center for Reproductive Health, Inc.*, 51 U.S.L.W. 4767 (U.S. June 15, 1983).
7. *Id.* at 4771.
8. *Id.* at 4776.
9. *Id.*
10. *Planned Parenthood, supra* note 5, at 69.
11. *Id.* at 71.
12. *Id.* at 70.
13. *Jones v. Smith*, 278 So.2d 339 (Fla. Dist. Ct. App.), *cert. denied*, 415 U.S. 958 (1974).
14. *Id.* at 344.
15. *See, e.g.*, Florida Medical Practice Act, FLA. STAT. ANN. §390.001 (4)(b).
16. *Charles v. Carey*, No. 79 C 4541 (N.D.Ill. Nov. 16, 1979) (an order granting a preliminary injunction), *aff'd in part, rev'd in part on other grounds*, 627 F.2d 772 (7th Cir. 1980).
17. FLA. STAT. ANN. §390.001(4)(b). In *Scheinberg v. Smith*, 659 F.2d 476 (5th Cir. 1981), the court upheld the constitutionality of the spousal notification provision noting that the Supreme Court in *Danforth, supra* note 5, at 52, had struck down a consent, not a notification, provision.
18. *H.L. v. Matheson*, 450 U.S. 398 (1981).
19. *Bellotti v. Baird*, 443 U.S. 622, 634 (1979) (*Bellotti II*). The Court in *Bellotti II* reviewed fairly extensively the cases involving the application of constitutional principles to minors. *Id.* at 633–39.
20. *Danforth, supra* note 5, at 74.
21. *Bellotti, supra* note 19, at 622.
22. *Id.* at 642.
23. *Id.* at 647–51.
24. *City of Akron, supra* note 6, at 4773.
25. *Bellotti, supra* note 19, at 643 n.23; *City of Akron, supra* note 6, at 4774.
26. MO. REV. STAT. §188.028.2; *Planned Parenthood Association v. Ashcroft*, 51 U.S.L.W. 4783 (U.S. June 15, 1983).

27. *Matheson, supra* note 18; UTAH CODE ANN. §76–7–304.
28. 450 U.S. at 407–413. In *Akron, supra* note 6, the Court noted that the "primary holding" in *Matheson, supra* note 18, was that the minor who had brought the suit did not have standing to challenge the statute on the grounds that it impermissibly burdened the rights of mature and emancipated minors, since she had not alleged that she herself was mature or emancipated. 51 U.S.L.W. at 4773 n.30.

Adoption

Can a single person adopt a child?

Yes. Every state has a statute defining who can adopt and the procedures involved, and every statute states that a single person may adopt.[1] Nonetheless, it is often not as easy for a single person to adopt as it is for a married couple. Social service and child welfare agencies frequently determine that it is in a child's best interests to have a two-parent family and may limit a single person to adopting a child unlikely to be adopted by anyone else. Some courts have also expressed a preference for a two-parent family in evaluating an adoption petition. A recent New York decision is a case in point. Although the judge found that adoptions "by single parents are no longer novel," he said that single-parent adoptions should be seen "as a very clear second choice to placement with two proper parents."[2] The court nevertheless permitted the adoption because the children were "hard-to-place" brothers and might be relegated to institutional care if the adoption were not permitted. Other courts have refused to allow a single person to adopt because of the adopter's widowed or separated status.[3] These rulings have held that permitting the adoption would not be in the child's best interests.[4]

Can unmarried cohabitants adopt a child?

The law is unclear. No state statute expressly prohibits adoption by unmarried couples. The limitations that often are applied to single people, however, are likely to apply to cohabiting singles. In addition, agencies and courts that review adoption petitions may consider an environment in which two people are living together without benefit of marriage as unsuitable for child rearing. Finally, every statute requires that both *spouses* join in an adoption petition.

Although no statute places this restriction on unmarried couples, social service and child welfare agencies that investigate the home environment for recommendations on adoption, are likely to require a cohabitant to consent to the adoption.

Can a gay person adopt a child?

Perhaps. By statute, only Florida prohibits adoption by a homosexual, providing, "No person eligible to adopt under this statute may adopt if that person is a homosexual."[5] Although there have been as yet no court challenges to this law, the statute might survive a challenge on constitutional grounds if in each case a court made findings of fact to determine what was in the child's best interests, rather than applying a per se restriction.

The limits on homosexual adoptions of children are likely to be at least as restrictive as those applied by agencies and courts to adoptions by singles and cohabitants.

Can a single adult adopt another adult?

Yes. No statute prohibits the adoption of an adult, but when a person is over a certain age, usually fourteen, his or her consent is required.[6] Adoption of an adult usually occurs when parties seek to create a certain legal and economic relationship. In this light the issue of adult adoption has arisen in the interpretation of wills and trust agreements. The language frequently used in wills and trusts refers to natural and adopted *children* or *issue*. Thus a number of courts have had to address the question of whether an adopted adult is legally the same as an adopted child for will or trust purposes. In four states (Kansas, Maryland, New Mexico, and New York)[7] adult adoptees can receive gifts given by a will or trust to adopted "children"; in New Jersey and Pennsylvania[8] they cannot; in California, Delaware, Iowa, and Kentucky there may be a legal presumption to include or exclude adult adoptees, but exceptions are permitted depending on circumstances defined by the courts.[9]

The issue of adult adoptions frequently comes before the courts in the context of adult homosexual adoptions.

Can a gay adult adopt another gay adult?

In some states. Although such adoptions are not prohibited by statute, except as just noted in Florida, courts have differed on whether to permit them. Typical of the rulings on both sides were those made by two New York courts in recent decisions. One court held that a thirty-two-year-old male could adopt a forty-three-year-old male so long as the purpose was not fraudulent or insincere, but rather to achieve economic, political, and social objectives.[10] The fact that the men were homosexual lovers was not considered a ground to deny the adoption petition. The standard, the court said, was obviously not the best interests of the child test, but rather whether the adoption would "promote the moral and temporal interests of the person to be adopted."[11] A different New York court denied the adoption petition of two men, saying that it was an attempt to substitute the adoption relationship for marriage, which was an impossibility; it revealed an intent to evade inheritance laws; and it did not represent a parent-child relationship, which is what the adoption laws are all about.[12]

NOTES

1. *See also* §3 of the Revised Uniform Adoption Act, which lists an unmarried adult as one of the persons who may adopt.
2. *In re Anthony R.*, 8 Fam. L. Rep. (BNA) 2062 (N.Y. Surr. Ct. Nov. 10, 1981).
3. *See, e.g., Bernhardt v. Lutheran Social Services*, 385 A.2d 1197 (Md. App. 1978) (separated); *Ross v. Dept. of Health & Rehabilitative Services*, 347 So.2d 753 (Fla. Ct. App. 1977) (widow and economic condition).
4. *See* the discussion of "best interests of child" standard in the section on custody, at   .
5. Fla. Stat. Ann. §63.042(3). This clause was a 1977 amendment to the adoption statute.
6. *See, e.g.,* Alaska Stat. §20.10.010 (age 14); Conn. Gen. Stat. Ann. §45-63 (age 14); Del. Code Ann. tit. 13 §903 (age 14); Me. Rev. Stat. Ann. tit. 19, §531 (age 14). *But see* Cal. Civ. Code §221 (age 12); Md. Ann. Code art. 16, §70 (age 10). *See also* Comment, "Adoption of Adults: A Family Law Anomaly," 54 *Cornell L. Rev.* 566 (1969).
7. *In re Estate of Fortney*, 611 P.2d 599 (Kan. App. 1980); *Evans v. McCoy*, 436 A.2d 436 (Md. App. 1981); *Delaney v. First National*

Bank, 386 P.2d 711 (N.M. 1963); *In re Trust of Simpson*, 395 N.Y.S.2d 917 (Sup. Ct. 1977).

8. *In re Estate of Nicol*, 377 A.2d 1201 (N.J. Super. 1977); *In re Estate of Tafel*, 296 A.2d 797 (Pa. 1972).

9. *In re Estate of Pittman*, 163 Cal. Rptr. 527 (Ct. App. 1980); *Chichester v. Wilmington Trust Co.*, 377 A.2d 11 (Del. 1977); *First National Bank v. Mackey*, 338 N.W.2d 361 (Iowa 1983); *Minary v. Citizens Fidelity Bank & Trust Co.*, 419 S.W.2d 340 (Ky. 1967).

10. *In re Adult Anonymous II*, 452 N.Y.S.2d 198, 200 (App. Div. 1982).

11. *Id.* at 199 [quoting *Stevens v. Halstead*, 168 N.Y.S. 142 (1917)].

12. *In re Robert P.*, 9 Fam. L. Rep. (BNA) 2267 (N.Y. Fam. Ct. Jan. 31, 1983).

Artificial Insemination

What is "artificial insemination"?

Artificial insemination means the introduction of semen from a woman's husband or another male by artificial means in order to induce pregnancy. It is estimated that at least 250,000 people in the United States have been conceived by artificial insemination.[1] The procedure is becoming more common today as the wait grows longer for adoptions. Not all of the legal issues involving artificial insemination are of concern to single people.

Is it lawful for a single woman to be artificially inseminated?

The law is unclear. Although single women have been artificially inseminated, there have been no reported cases on the issue. At least 25 states have statutes defining and regulating artificial insemination.[2] Of these, only the Georgia and Oregon statutes provide for artificial insemination for single women. The Georgia statute permits artificial insemination to be performed by a licensed doctor "upon any female human being." The Oregon law provides that artificial insemination can only be performed on a woman with her written consent, *or if married*, with the written consent of the husband as well.

Most of the statutes as well as the Uniform Parentage Act refer only to married women and might be interpreted to preclude insemination of single women. In Oklahoma, for example, although the statute is silent on the subject of single women, the attorney general recently issued an opinion saying that Oklahoma law does not allow an unmarried woman to be artificially inseminated.[3]

Some doctors may refuse to inseminate artificially a single woman because of a value judgment they make regarding the desirability of two-parent families. Some may also refuse because of uncertainty about the legality of the procedure on singles. Single women who have been artificially inseminated have frequently found help and information regarding doctors who will perform the procedures on singles, from local women's groups and women's health centers.[4]

What legal arguments support a single woman's right to artificial insemination?

There are several constitutional arguments that can be made. The United States Supreme Court has held that certain rights regarding procreation,[5] contraception,[6] childbirth,[7] and abortion[8] are constitutionally protected. In *Eisenstadt v. Baird*, for example, the Court extended to single people the right of privacy regarding matters of contraception, holding that if "the right of privacy means anything, it is the right of the *individual*, married or single, to be free from unwanted governmental intrusions into matters so fundamentally affecting a person as the decision whether to bear or beget a child."[9] In addition, since criminal laws are often strictly construed, unless a statute specifically prohibits single women from being artificially inseminated, an argument can be made that no legal sanctions should exist against their so doing. Some analysts who reject artificial insemination for single women argue that it is not in the child's best interests to be raised by a single woman.[10] This argument has been rejected by every state, since every state by statute permits singles to adopt.[11]

Does the donor of semen have any rights or obligations toward the child conceived through artificial insemination?

In most states, no. The non-husband semen donor is treated in law as if he is not the natural father and has no rights, obligations, or interest with respect to the child born as a result of artificial insemination.[12] Usually the donor is anonymous, which is added insurance that there will be no questions of rights or duties. Rather, the statutes provide that the husband with whose consent the woman was artificially inseminated is to be regarded as the father of the child.[13] One exception is the Washington statute, which provides that the donor shall not be considered the natural father of the child unless both the donor and the woman agree to this in writing.[14]

In one case, *C.M. v. C.C.*,[15] the donor wished to be known, asserted his paternity and desire of providing support and requested visitation rights. The man, C.M., and the woman, C.C., although friends, were never married and had not lived together. After the birth of the child, C.M. sued to gain visitation rights and won. Generally, the unwed natural father can assert his paternity, assume support obligations and gain visitation or even custody rights. The question for the court in this case was whether to define C.M. as the natural father, since conception was not accomplished through "natural" means. As there was no dispute as to the identity of the donor, the court equated C.M.'s position with that of a husband who was the donor for his wife's artificial insemination. Since a husband would be considered the father for purposes of rights and obligations, the court held that C.M. was the "natural" father and therefore entitled to visitation rights.

If a husband and wife who have had a child by artificial insemination are divorced, does the husband have rights or responsibilities toward the child?

Yes. With regard to responsibilities, the courts that have addressed this issue have found that by consenting to the artificial insemination procedure, the husband assumed permanent duties of fatherhood.[16] In a leading case on this issue the California Supreme Court held that the word *father* in the support statute meant lawful father, not just biological father,[17] and that after divorce the ex-husband had a duty to support the child. Even when state statutes have required the written consent of the husband to the procedure, courts have found that oral consent suffices to impose support obligations on the husband after divorce.[18]

Upon divorce, a parent generally has a right to prevent the adoption of his or her child unless the parental rights have been terminated because of abuse, abandonment, or neglect.[19] In at least one case a court has held that a divorced husband who consented to the artificial insemination of his wife has the right to prevent the adoption of the child by his ex-wife's new husband.[20]

NOTES

1. Kritchevsky, "The Unmarried Woman's Right to Artificial Insemination: A Call for an Expanded Definition of Family," 4 *Harv. Women's L. J.* 1 at n.3 (1981).

2. ALASKA. STAT. §20.20.010; ARK. STAT. ANN. §61–141(c); CAL. CIV. CODE §7005; COLO. REV. STAT. §19–6–106; CONN. GEN. STAT. §§45–69f to 69n; FLA. STAT. §742.11; GA. CODE ANN. §19–721; 43–34–42; IDAHO CODE §39–5401; KAN. STAT. ANN. §§23–128–130; LA. CIV. CODE ANN. art. 188; MD. EST. & TRUSTS CODE ANN. §1–206(b); MICH. COMP. LAWS ANN. §§333.2824, 700.11; MINN. STAT. ANN. §257.56; MONT. CODE ANN. §40–6–106; NEV. REV. STAT. §126.061; N.Y. DOM. REL. LAW §73; N.C. GEN. STAT. §49A–1; OKLA. STAT. ANN. tit. 10, §§551–553; OR. REV. STAT. §§109.239–.247; TENN. CODE ANN. §53–446; TEX. FAM. CODE ANN. tit. 12, §12.03; VA. CODE §64.1–7.1; WASH. REV. CODE ANN. §26.26.050; WIS. STAT. ANN. §§767.47(a), 891.40(1); WYO. STAT. §14–2–103.

3. Opinion No. 83–162, 9 Fam. L. Rep. (BNA) 2761 (Sept. 29, 1983).

4. For sample artificial insemination contracts between private parties, see Davies, "Artificial Insemination," in *Women's Rights: Law Practice and Advocacy* (Clark-Boardman), forthcoming.

5. *Skinner v. Oklahoma*, 316 U.S. 535 (1942).

6. *Carey v. Population Services International*, 431 U.S. 678 (1977); *Eisenstadt v. Baird*, 405 U.S. 435 (1972).

7. *Zablocki v. Redhail*, 434 U.S. 374 (1978) (dictum: women have a fundamental right to bear a child even if it's illegitimate).

8. *Roe v. Wade*, 410 U.S. 113 (1973).

9. *Eisenstadt*, *supra* note 6 at 453.

10. *See, e.g.*, Jensen, "Artificial Insemination and the Law," (1982) *B.Y.U. L. Rev.* 935.

11. *See* the section on adoption at page 89. For a further discussion of the rights of single women, *see* Kritchevsky, "Unmarried Woman's Right to Artificial Insemination," *supra* note 1; Comment, "Artificial Insemination and Surrogate Motherhood—A Nursery Full of Unresolved Questions," 17 *Williamette L. Rev.* 913 (1981).

12. *See, e.g.*, OR. REV. STAT. §109.239.

13. *Id*.

14. WASH. REV. CODE ANN. §26.26.050(2).

15. 377 A.2d 821 (N.J. Super. 1977)

16. *R.S. v. R.S.*, 10 Fam. L. Rep. (BNA) 1052 (Kan. Ct. App. Oct. 27, 1983); *K.S. v. G.S.*, 440 A.2d 64 (N.J. Super. 1981); *People v. Sorenson*, 437 P.2d 495 (Cal. 1968); *Gursky v. Gursky*, 242 N.Y.S.2d 406 (Sup. Ct. 1963).

17. *Sorenson, supra* note 16.

18. *R.S. v. R.S., supra* note 16; *K.S. v. G.S., supra* note 16.

19. See ACLU Handbook, *The Rights of Parents*, by A. Sussman and M. Guggenheim (1980).

20. *In re Adoption of Anonymous*, 345 N.Y.S.2d 430 (Surr. Ct. 1973).

Custody and Visitation

Custody generally refers to the responsibilities of maintaining and nurturing your child, and involves the right to make decisions regarding your child. Usually a parent has custody of a child from birth until the child is no longer a minor. The United States Supreme Court has described a parent's interest in retaining custody as "substantial,"[1] and held that

> it is plain that the interest of a parent in the companionship, care, custody and management of his or her children "come[s] to this Court with a momentum for respect lacking when appeal is made to liberties which derive merely from shifting economic arrangements."[2]

Nonetheless, courts sometimes terminate a parent's custody primarily for reasons of abuse, abandonment, or neglect. Every state has statutory provisions setting forth grounds and procedures for terminating parental rights.[3]

When parents are divorced or separated, the child or children live with the custodial parent. The other parent has visitation rights—that is, rights to see the child for specific periods of time, which can be set by agreement between the parents or court-ordered. Today, joint custody is becoming more common, whereby both parents have equal legal rights and responsibilities, for example, making decisions regarding a child's education or religious training. It does not necessarily mean that both parents have physical custody, which is the right and responsibility to maintain the principal home and to provide routine care for the child.[4] One parent alone may have physical custody, or both parents may alternate.

Custody decisions are made either by agreement or by courts after trial. Trial courts generally have broad discretion in custody matters, and appellate courts will not overturn a lower court's decision unless it finds an abuse of that discretion, or a decision that is "clearly erroneous." Once a court is involved in custody questions, it retains jurisdiction over the issue; that is, a custody decision can be modified or changed so long as a child remains a minor.

What standards do judges use to decide custody cases?

The standard generally applied in state statutes is the "best interests of the child."[5] Some statutes list criteria to be considered in awarding custody, such as—

1. the age and sex of the child;
2. the relationship of the child with the parent or parents;
3. the child's interaction with the environment of the home, school, and larger community;
4. the mental and physical health of all the parties;
5. the child's wishes.[6]

Some statutes require an examination of economic factors— employment and earning capacity, for example—in determining custody issues,[7] and others include amorphous criteria, such as the "moral fitness" of the parents or their capacity to give love and affection.[8]

What are the limitations of the best interests test?

The problem with the best interests test is that although it sounds reasonable, in application it is often a vague standard that leaves room for judicial expression of bias; for example, judges who think a parent's church attendance is important to a child's development may use that as a factor in awarding custody; and judges who disapprove of a "bohemian" life-style may award custody to the parent with the more traditional job and home life.[9] The possibilities of judicial prejudice are manifold. In one case a court expressed a preference for country living and church attendance over city living (and presumably atheism), and awarded custody accordingly.[10] In a well-known case in which the judge gave full rein to his biases, he concluded that one of the homes

> provides [the child] with a stable, dependable, conventional, middle-class, middlewest background and an opportunity for a college education and profession, if he desires it. It provides a solid foundation and secure atmosphere. In the [other] home, [the child] would have more freedom of conduct and thought with an opportunity to develop his individual talents. It would be more exciting and challenging in many respects, but romantic, impractical and unstable.[11]

The court noted that there was no question of unfitness, but rather it was making an assessment of what was best for the child. Custody was awarded to the party with the middle-class, midwest background.

Other courts may be as biased, but they are likely to be less blatant. The United States Supreme Court, although it has not ruled on the issue directly, has said that it would be a violation of the due process clause "[i]f a state were to attempt to force the breakup of a natural family, over the objection of the parents and their children, without some showing of unfitness and for the sole reason that to do so was thought to be in the children's best interests."[12] This was stated in the context of an adoption proceeding and a termination of parental rights. It is not certain that the reasoning would be applied to custody cases, which involve rights and duties in child care, not the termination of all rights and duties.

Is there a preference for mothers in awarding custody?

There is no clear answer today. There is a doctrine or policy called the tender years preference. In one classic formulation of the doctrine, a court held, "[I]t is well-known by all men that no other love is quite so tender, no other solicitude quite so deep, no other devotion quite so enduring as that of a mother."[13] The emergence of this preference was a swing of the pendulum away from the nineteenth-century precept that a father had an absolute, virtually a property, right to his children;[14] mothers could be awarded custody only upon a showing of severe unfitness of a father. Through the efforts of the women's movement in the mid-nineteenth century, women began to secure property and economic rights and expand their educational opportunities. Of fundamental concern to these early feminists was the battle to gain custody rights. The law mirrored these social and political changes and a maternal preference in the custody of young children of tender years evolved. By the beginning of the twentieth century, there was an almost universal acceptance of maternal preference.

By the mid-twentieth century the pendulum began to swing back as more and more states and courts adopted the best interests of the child standard. Today most statutes are gender-neutral in their language; some openly prohibit a presumption in favor of one parent, and state that fathers and mothers are to be treated equally.[15] At least twenty-six states and the District of Columbia have rejected the tender years doctrine by statute.[16] In addition, high courts in several states have declared the doctrine a violation of either the state or federal constitutions, or contrary to the intent of the state statute or the best interests standard.[17]

Do any courts still apply the tender years doctrine in making custody decisions?

Yes. Some courts have held that in determining the best interests of the child, maternal preference for custody of a young child or infant is one of several factors to be considered.[18] Some courts use the doctrine as a "tie-breaker." A recent formulation of this was in a Florida case in which the court said that "other essential factors being equal, the mother of the infant of tender years should receive prime consideration for custody."[19] Most recently the Mississippi Supreme Court reaffirmed the tender years doctrine even though it noted that the policy had undergone "a weakening process" in other jurisdictions.[20] The court said that the Mississippi statute, which states that neither parent has paramount right concerning custody,[21] makes the best interests of the child test the cardinal principle to be considered. In this context, the child's age and a maternal preference for a young child are factors to be considered in determining the best interests.

Thus some courts, while no longer using the tender years doctrine as a legal presumption, are incorporating it into a factual determination of a child's best interests.

Is there a hidden sex-based preference in the best interests test?

Some lawyers involved in custody questions say yes. They believe that mothers frequently are discriminated against in the application of the best interests standard.[22] Although women have custody of their children in nearly 90 percent of the instances of marital breakup, in the vast majority of these cases custody was not in dispute, since the fathers did not want custody. According to a recent study, women are losing two-thirds of the litigated custody cases.[23]

There appear to be several reasons for this, one of which is economic. As courts review the facts to determine the best interests of the child, they frequently assess the economic and job situations of the parents. Women, individually and as a group, have considerably fewer financial resources than men. According to 1980 census data, families maintained by women had a median yearly income of $10,830, whereas families headed by men had a median income of $18,775.[24] Many women have stayed at home to raise children and have had little or no experience in the job market; those who have worked outside the home have less earning power than men. Thus, giving significant weight to financial resources tends to discriminate against mothers. Some state statutes specifically require a review of economic factors.[25] In other instances, courts assessed each parent's financial situation and found that, among other factors, the greater economic resources of the fathers created an environment best for the child in question.[26] Women who find themselves in a situation of unequal economic resources vis-à-vis their former husbands should argue, as one case recently holds,[27] that differences in financial situations should not be of major significance, since the issue of custody is separate and distinct from the duty to support through both alimony and child support funds.

Women also may suffer from the application of a double standard regarding employment. It is appropriate, indeed socially mandatory, that a father work, and men's work is generally understood to be outside the home. When a mother works outside the home there are questions about whether she is properly meeting her domestic obligations.

It is not unusual, for example, for a judge to conclude that since a working mother had to have baby-sitters, there were strains placed on the parental relationship with the child. The fact that the father also worked outside the home and had some other person to care for the child during the day was not deemed a negative factor.[28]

Insofar as there is a judicial preference for the nuclear family rather than single heads of households, women are at a disadvantage. They remarry at about sixty percent of the rate of divorced men.[29] This is frequently an issue in a court proceeding to modify a custody award after the father has remarried.[30] Although a minority view, one recent Pennsylvania case held that the lower court was erroneous in ruling that a two-parent family is favored by law.[31]

Finally, although not directly related to the best interests test, mothers are often burdened because husbands frequently threaten to seek custody to gain financial concessions regarding alimony and child support.[32] Indeed one court recently acknowledged the practice. The court refused to set aside a property settlement that the wife claimed she had agreed to only after the husband had threatened to contest custody, saying, "The facts are that custody is frequently a bargaining chip in settlement negotiations whether we like it or not."[33]

Is there a true sex-neutral standard for awarding custody?

Yes. It's called the primary caretaker standard, and it is a gender-neutral replacement of the tender years doctrine and a refinement of the best interests of the child standard. The primary caretaker standard is a recognition of the fact that in most families one of the parents is likely to assume responsibility for daily plans, preparations, and provision of necessities. Recently some courts have begun to recognize that failure to give positive consideration to the primary caretaker "ignores the benefits likely to flow to the child from maintaining day-to-day contact with the parent on whom the child has depended for satisfying his physical and psychological needs."[34] A West Virginia court listed factors that identified a primary caretaker.

- preparing and planning meals
- bathing, grooming, and dressing
- purchasing, cleaning, and care of clothes
- medical care: nursing and trips to the doctor
- arranging for social interaction after school
- arranging alternative care (baby-sitting)
- putting to bed, attending during night, awakening in morning
- discipline, manners, toilet training
- education; and religious, cultural, and social training
- teaching elementary skills: reading, writing, and arithmetic[35]

These are gender-neutral roles that either the mother or father can fulfill. Courts should not necessarily base a custody award solely on a determination of who is the primary caretaker, since couples may agree to assume different roles in working out living arrangements for themselves. Nonetheless, the best interests of the child standard would seem to require serious consideration of this factor to minimize disruption in a young child's routine.

Can a single person cohabiting with another lose custody of her or his child?

Yes. Judges differ, however, and state courts have viewed cohabitation in different ways, more or less favorably to the cohabitant. A brief overview of the range of court opinions will give you an idea of what arguments you may be up against as well as what arguments you can make in support of your situation.

Some courts have held that cohabitation is a sign of immorality and indicates that a parent cannot provide the proper moral training for a child.[36] In a leading case espousing this position, the Illinois Supreme Court acknowledged that there was no showing that the children had been harmed, but it found that the possibility of future harm was significant. The court said that the cohabitant's "disregard for existing standards of conduct instructs her children, by example, that they, too, may ignore [the state's moral standards] and could well encourage the children to engage in similar activity in the future."[37] Cases that follow this reasoning presume without requiring factual support that a single cohabiting parent is unfit and that children will inevitably be harmed by the parent's conduct. In contrast, sometimes a judge will find that a little bit of "immorality" such as a weekend visit by a lover is tolerable so long as it does not constitute flagrant, open, and continuous cohabitation.[38]

Other state courts have held that cohabitation is only one of several factors to consider in assessing the best interests of the child.[39] A few have held that cohabitation is irrelevant unless there is a showing of actual harm to the child.[40] Although requiring a showing of harm offers the cohabiting parent more protection than merely considering cohabitation as one of several factors, both approaches mean that, at a minimum, a court cannot use extramarital cohabitation or sexual relations alone to determine which parent should retain custody. One court held: "an award of custody is not a tool to regulate human behavior"; the court's only object is to find the best interests of the child.[41] The Alaska Supreme Court's explanation for reversing a lower court's change of custody from the mother to the father is a concise statement of why courts should reject considerations of "immorality" in making custody determinations.

> [W]e cannot countenance the court's reference to the mother's sexual conduct. Whether intended as condemnatory of the mother's sexual conduct or only as indicative of the mother's unstable life-style, our concern is that the mother's bearing of children out of wedlock or her instability in terms of relationships should be determinative only were such conduct to adversely affect the child or the mother's parenting abilities. . . . To avoid even the suggestion that a custody award stems from a life-style conflict between a trial judge and a parent, we reiterate that trial courts must scrupulously avoid reference to such factors absent evidence of an adverse effect to the parent-child relationship.[42]

Can courts place limits on extramarital sexual behavior in making custody and visitation decisions?

Yes, and they have. In a recent Illinois case, a court said that the mother could retain custody of the children only if she married her lover or broke off with him.[43] The court also said that if the father did not stop criticizing the mother's behavior to the children he might lose visitation rights. In several cases courts have said that a single parent could not have overnight visitation with the children if a companion of the opposite sex was present.[44]

Some courts have refused to impose restrictions on the grounds that they are (1) vague, overbroad, and incapable of enforcement;[45] (2) an abuse of a trial court's discretion;[46] or (3) improper inasmuch as the child was not harmed.[47] Restrictions are most frequently imposed in cases involving homosexual relationships.

Have courts denied custody to a single parent because he or she is homosexual?

Yes. Although, lesbian mothers and homosexual fathers have begun to win some custody battles, the majority of courts still award custody to nonhomosexual parents. Some judges deny custody to a lesbian mother or gay father because they deem homosexuality immoral. One court, expressing a reluctance to discuss the issue, never mentioned the fact that the mother was a lesbian, merely noting that the subject is "beyond the pale of the most permissive society."[48]

Some courts find that homosexuality by definition creates a change of circumstances sufficient to change custody,[49] while others raise the specter of social opprobrium to deny custody.[50] Some courts find that the child will be harmed by living with a homosexual parent. Frequently these courts have presumed harm, since no evidence of damage was shown.[51] Finally, some courts have awarded custody to the nonhomosexual parent charging that the homosexual parents placed their interests above that of the children because they wanted to continue their relationships with their lovers.[52]

Have any courts granted custody or visitation rights to a homosexual parent?

Yes. Courts in at least eleven states have held that custody or visitation rights cannot be denied simply because of sexual preference.[53] Basically these courts reason that sexual preference is relevant to custody questions only if there is evidence of some harm to the child. In other words, these courts state that homosexuality "does not *ipso facto* constitute unfitness for custody."[54] One court went so far as to say that sexual preference by itself is irrelevant to a consideration of parenting skills.[55]

In two unusual cases courts have awarded custody to lesbians who were not related to the children. In one case, the child's mother had given up custody to a lesbian woman with the understanding that the woman eventually would adopt the child. Two years later a court denied the natural mother's petition to get the child back. The lesbian had been the child's custodian and "psychological parent" and the court found the child "well adjusted and receiving excellent care."[56] In the second case, a court granted custody to the deceased mother's lesbian lover rather than to a married aunt.[57]

Have courts placed restrictions on custody or visitation rights because of the parent's homosexuality?

Yes. Courts have placed various limits on homosexual parents. Some have ordered the parent to discontinue any relationship with a lover;[58] others have only required that the parent not live with a lover.[59] Some courts have said that a lover cannot be in the home when the child is there.[60] Still others have held that the child cannot stay with the noncustodial parent overnight;[61] some courts have said that an overnight visit may be allowed but a lover cannot be present.[62] One court ordered a parent not to take the child to social gatherings where gay activists are present, or to services in a gay church.[63]

Can sexual involvement or cohabitation with a person of another race affect custody rights?

Only a few courts have changed an award of custody because of interracial relationships. In one case a white mother who had custody of her children was having an affair with a black man. Although the trial court changed custody to the father, the appellate court reversed, saying that the mother had demonstrated care and love for the children and that there was no reason to take custody from her.[64] In another case, a white mother who had custody lived with and then married a black man. The court took her child from her saying that the child would inevitably suffer social stigma because of the interracial cohabitation and subsequent marriage.[65] In a unanimous opinion, The Supreme Court recently reversed the lower court in this second case, ruling that the change of custody was a violation of the Fourteenth Amendment of the Constitution. The Court held that "[t]he

effects of racial prejudice, however real, cannot justify...
removing an infant child from the custody of its natural
mother," if she has been found fit to have custody.[66]

**In a custody dispute does a record of wife-beating
automatically lead to the father's loss of custody?**

No. Courts sometimes ignore the father's violence toward the mother so long as it was not directed at, or done in
front of, the child. In one extreme example, a father was
allowed to retain custody of his children even though he had
killed the mother by stabbing her twenty-two times. The
court seemed affected by the fact that the murder was not
done in the children's presence.[67] In a recent, more rationally
decided case, an Indiana court considered the fact that the
father beat the mother even though the child did not see or
know of it. The court said that the father's conduct indicated
a potential for violence and physical harm such that it was in
the child's best interests to remove him from the potentially
harmful environment.[68]

How widespread is the practice of joint custody?

At least twenty-eight states by statute have authorized
awards of joint custody.[69] In other states some judges have
ordered joint custody by finding that it is in the best interests
of the child.

**Do both parents have to agree to joint custody before it
is ordered?**

In Illinois, Kansas, Louisiana, Massachusetts, Ohio, Texas,
and Wisconsin the statutes require that both parents have to
agree. In several states (including Iowa, Michigan, New
Jersey, and Pennsylvania) courts have ordered joint custody
when not requested or over the objection of one parent.[70]

An order of joint custody is most likely to be carried out
when both parties agree to it. In fact, when the parents,
although separated, are cooperating in the upbringing of their
children, an order is not really necessary. The potential for
problems is clear when parents have not wanted to share
custody and were so ordered.[71]

NOTES

1. *Stanley v. Illinois*, 405 U.S. 645, 652 (1972).
2. *Id.* at 651 [quoting *Kovacs v. Cooper*, 336 U.S. 77, 95 (1949) (Frankfurter, J., concurring)].
3. *See* the discussion of termination of parental rights in the ACLU Handbook, *The Rights of Parents* by A. Sussman and M. Guggenheim, (1980).
4. *See, e.g.*, IOWA CODE §598.1(4)(5).
5. *See, e.g.*, COLO. REV. STAT. §19–3–109; MD. CTS. & JUD. PROC. CODE ANN. §3–831(3); OR. REV. STAT. §419.507; WYO. STAT. ANN §14–2–307(a).
6. *See, e.g.*, ILL. REV. STAT. ch. 40 §101–802.
7. *See, e.g.*, FLA. STAT. ANN. §61.13; N.D. CENT. CODE ANN. §14–09–06.2; VT. STAT. ANN. tit. 15, §557.
8. *See, e.g.*, FLA. STAT. ANN. §61.13; MICH. COMP. LAWS ANN. §722.23(3)(a)(b).
9. *See, e.g.*, *Painter v. Bannister*, 140 N.W.2d 152 (Iowa 1966).
10. *Shaw v. Shaw*, 462 S.W.2d 222 (Ark. 1971).
11. *Painter*, *supra* note 9, at 154.
12. *Quilloin v. Walcott*, 434 U.S. 246, 256 (1978) [citing *Smith v. Organization of Foster Families*, 431 U.S. 816, 863 (1977)].
13. *Ellis v. Johnson*, 260 S.W. 1010, 1012 (Mo. Ct. App. 1924).
14. *See, e.g.*, *State v. Richardson*, 40 N.H. 272 (1860).
15. *See, e.g.*, OHIO REV. CODE ANN. §3109.03.
16. ALASKA STAT. §09.55.205(2); ARIZ. REV. STAT. ANN. §25–332(D); CAL. CIV. CODE §4600(b)(1); COLO. REV. STAT. §14–10–124(3); DEL. CODE ANN. tit. 13, §722(b); D.C. CODE ANN. §16–911(a)(5); GA. CODE ANN. §74–10(a); HAWAII REV. STAT §571–46(1); IND. CODE ANN. §31–1–11.5–21(a); KAN. STAT. ANN. §60–1610(b); LA. CIV. CODE ANN. art. 157(A); MASS. GEN. LAWS ANN. ch. 208, §31; MINN. STAT. ANN. §518.17(3); MO. ANN. STAT. §452.150; NEB. REV. STAT. §42–364(2); NEV. REV. STAT. §125.140(1); N.H. REV. STAT. ANN. §458:17(VI); N.J. REV. STAT. §9:2–4; N.Y. DOM. REL. LAW §240(1); N.C. GEN. STAT. §50–13.2(a); N.D. CENT. CODE §14–09–06; OHIO REV. CODE ANN. §3109.03; OR. REV. STAT. §107.137(3); S.D. CODIFIED LAWS ANN. §30–27–19(2); WASH. REV. CODE ANN. §26.16.125; W. VA. CODE §48–2–15; WYO. STAT. §20–2–113(a).
17. *See, e.g.*, *Devine v. Devine*, 398 So. 2d 686 (Ala. 1981) (federal constitution); *Johnson v. Johnson*, 564 P.2d 71 (Alaska 1977) (statutory intent); *In re Marriage of Bowen*, 219 N.W.2d 683 (Iowa 1974) (best

interests); *Spriggs v. Carson*, 368 A.2d 635 (Pa. 1977) (state constitution).

18. *See, e.g., Jensen v. Jensen*, 597 P.2d 733 (Mont. 1979).

19. *Kershner v. Crocker*, 400 So. 2d 126, 127 (Fla. Dist. Ct. App. 1981) (citations omitted).

20. *Albright v. Albright*, 10 Fam. L. Rep. (BNA) 1005 (Miss. Sept. 21, 1983).

21. MISS. CODE ANN. §93–13–1.

22. *See, e.g.*, Woods, Been, and Schulman, "Sex and Economic Discrimination in Child Custody Awards," 16 *Clearinghouse Rev.* 1130 (1982) (available from the National Center on Women and Family Law, 799 Broadway, Rm. 402, New York, NY 10003, (212) 697–8200); Polikoff, "Why Are Mothers Losing: A Brief Analysis of Criteria Used in Child Custody Determinations," 7 *Women's Rts. L. Rep.* 235 (1982); Polikoff, "Child Custody Disputes: Exploding the Myth that Mothers Always Win," to be published in Diamond, ed., *Families, Politics and Public Policy: A Feminist Dialogue on Women and the State*. *See also* Weitzman and Dixon, "Child Custody Awards: Legal Standards and Empirical Patterns for Child Custody, Support and Visitation After Divorce," 12 *U.C.D. L. Rev.* 472 (1979); Uviller, "Fathers' Rights and Feminism: The Maternal Presumption Revisited," 1 *Harv. Women's L. J.* 107 (1978).

23. Weitzman and Dixon, *"Child Custody Awards," supra* note 22.

24. Figures cited in Woods, Been, and Schulman, *Child Custody Awards," supra* note 22.

25. *See, e.g.*, FLA. STAT. ANN. §61.13; N.D. CENT. CODE ANN. §14–09–06.2; VT. STAT. ANN. tit. 15, §557.

26. *See, e.g., Perkins v. Perkins*, 589 S.W.2d 588 (Ark. Ct. App. 1979); *McCreery v. McCreery*, 237 S.E.2d 167 (Va. 1977).

27. *Albright, supra* note 20.

28. *See, e.g., Durrette v. Durrette*, 288 S.E.2d 432 (Va. 1982). *See also*, Polikoff, "Why Are Mothers Losing," *supra* note 22, Woods, Been, and Schulman, "Sex and Economic Discrimination," *supra* note 22.

29. National Center for Health Statistics, cited in Woods, Been, and Schulman, "Sex and Economic Discrimination," *supra* note 22, at n.5 and accompanying text.

30. *See, e.g., Simmons v. Simmons*, 576 P.2d 589 (Kan. 1978). *See* the discussion in Woods, Been, and Schulman, "Sex and Economic Discrimination," *supra* note 22, at 1132–33.

31. *Jordan v. Jordan*, 448 A.2d 1113 (Pa. Super. Ct. 1982).

32. Polikoff, *supra* note 22, cited in Woods, Been, and Schulman, "Sex and Economic Discrimination" *supra* note 22, at 1134.

33. *In re Marriage of Lawrence*, 642 P.2d 1043, 1049 (Mont. 1982).

34. *Jordan, supra* note 31, at 1115.

35. *Garska v. McCoy*, 278 S.E.2d 357, 363 (W. Va. 1981).

36. *See, e.g., Ryan v. Ryan*, 652 S.W.2d 313 (Mo. Ct. App. 1983); *Jarrett v. Jarrett*, 400 N.E.2d 421 (Ill. 1979), *cert. denied*, 449 U.S. 927

(1980). (Brennan, J. dissented, saying that the Illinois court had conclusively presumed that cohabitation adversely affected the children.)

37. *Jarrett, supra* note 36, at 424. Several Illinois cases after *Jarrett* have attempted to limit the impact of *Jarrett*. *See, e.g., In re Marriage of Olson*, 424 N.E.2d 386 (Ill. App. Ct. 1981); *Thompson v. Thompson*, 9 Fam. L. Rep. (BNA) 2437 (Ill. Oct. 25, 1983).

38. *Willcutts v. Willcutts*, 410 N.E.2d 1057 (Ill. App. Ct. 1980).

39. *See, e.g., In re Wellman*, 6 Fam. L. Rep. (BNA) 2544 (Cal. Ct. App. April 24, 1980); *In re Marriage of Kramer*, 397 N.W.2d 359 (Iowa 1980); *Ahlman v. Ahlman*, 267 N.W.2d 521 (Neb. 1978); *Lapp v. Lapp*, 9 Fam. L. Rep. (BNA) 2606 (N.D. July 14, 1983); *Ryser v. Ryser*, 9 Fam. L. Rep. (BNA) 2639 (Okla. Ct. App. July 26, 1983).

40. Alaska: *Craig v. McBride*, 639 P.2d 303 (Alaska 1982); Colorado: *In re Marriage of Moore*, 531 P.2d 995 (Colo. Ct. App. 1975); Illinois: *Thompson, supra* note 37; Louisiana: *Cleeton v. Cleeton*, 383 So. 2d 1231 (La. 1980); Massachusetts: *Fort v. Fort*, 7 Fam. L. Rep. (BNA) 2750 (Mass. App. Ct. Sept. 11, 1981); Mississippi: *Kavanaugh v. Carraway*, 9 Fam. L. Rep. (BNA) 2668 (Miss. Aug. 3, 1983); Ohio: *In re Burrell*, 388 N.E.2d 738 (Ohio 1979); Pennsylvania: *H.H. v. L.H.*, 439 A.2d 187 (Pa. Super. Ct. 1981). *See also* Uniform Marriage and Divorce Act, §402 ("The court shall not consider conduct of a proposed custodian that does not affect his relationship to the child.")

41. *Cleeton, supra* note 40.

42. *Craig, supra* note 40, at 306.

43. *Krabel v. Krabel*, 429 N.E.2d 1105 (Ill. App. Ct. 1981).

44. *See, e.g., Drum v. Drum*, 397 A.2d 1192 (Pa. 1979); *Palmer v. Palmer*, 416 A.2d 143 (Vt. 1980).

45. *Beaman v. Beaman*, 393 So. 2d 19 (Fla. Dist. Ct. App. 1980) (the order was that "no act of immorality" shall occur during visitation); *Dile v. Dile*, 426 A.2d 137 (Pa. Super. Ct. 1981) (the order prohibited visitation in the presence of an unrelated adult male; the appellate court narrowed to apply to one particular person).

46. *Draper v. Draper*, 7 Fam. L. Rep. (BNA) 2208 (Fla. Dist. Ct. App. Dec. 24, 1980) (abuse to order wife to marry lover if she wants to have custody).

47. *Sorace v. Sorace*, 344 A.2d 553 (Pa. Super. Ct. 1975).

48. *Spence v. Durham*, 198 S.E.2d 537, 541 (N.C. 1973).

49. *Newsome v. Newsome*, 256 S.E.2d 849 (N.C. Ct. App. 1979).

50. *Jacobson v. Jacobson*, 314 N.W.2d 78 (N.D. 1981) (social mores and lack of legal recognition of status of relationship mean it is not in child's best interest to be with a homosexual parent); *S. v. S.*, 608 S.W.2d 64 (Ky. Ct. App. 1980), *cert. denied*, 451 U.S. 911 (1981) (child will bear the burden of teasing, possible harassment, and internal conflicts).

51. *S. v. S., supra* note 50 (potential for endangering child's welfare); *In re Jane B.*, 380 N.Y.S. 2d 848 (Sup. Ct. 1976) (conclusion without

110

evidence that the child was emotionally disturbed because of the mother's sexual preference).

52. *Jacobson v. Jacobson*, 314 N.W.2d 78 (N.D. 1981); *Hall v. Hall*, 6 Fam. L. Rep. (BNA) 2537 (Mich. Ct. App. Mar. 21, 1980).

53. California: *In re Lisa T.*, 7 Fam. L. Rep. (BNA) 2496 (Cal. Ct. App. Apr. 29, 1981); *Nadler v. Superior Court*, 63 Cal. Rptr. 352 (Ct. App. 1967); Colorado: *In re Hatzopoulos*, 4 Fam. L. Rep. (BNA) 2075 (Colo. Juv. Ct. July 8, 1977); Indiana: *D.H. v. J.H.*, 418 N.E.2d 286 (Ind. App. 1981); Massachusetts: *Bezio v. Patenaude*, 410 N.E.2d 1207 (Mass. 1980); New Jersey: *In re J.S. & C.*, 324 A.2d 90 (N.J. Super. Ct. 1974), *aff'd* 362 A.2d 54 (Super. 1976); New York: *DiStefano v. DiStefano*, 401 N.Y.S.2d 636 (App. Div. 1978); Oregon: *A. v. A.*, 514 P.2d 358 (Or. Ct. App. 1973); Utah: *Kallas v. Kallas*, 614 P.2d 641 (Utah 1980); Vermont: *Medeiros v. Medeiros*, 8 Fam. L. Rep. (BNA) 2372 (Vt. Super. Ct. Apr. 2, 1982); Virginia: *Doe v. Doe*, 284 S.E.2d 799 (Va. 1981); Washington: *Cabalquinto v. Cabalquinto*, 669 P.2d 886 (Wash. 1983).

54. *Werneburg v. Werneburg*, 6 Fam. L. Rep. (BNA) 2280 (N.Y. Fam. Ct. Jan. 29, 1980).

55. *Bezio v. Patenaude*, 410 N.E.2d 1207 (Mass. 1980).

56. *In re Lisa T.*, *supra* note 53.

57. *In re Hatzopoulos*, *supra* note 53.

58. *N.K.M. v. L.E.M.*, 616 S.W.2d 179 (Mo. Ct. App. 1980).

59. *Schuster v. Schuster*, 585 P.2d 130 (Wash. 1978).

60. *L. v. D.*, 630 S.W.2d 240 (Mo. Ct. App. 1982); *Woodruff v. Woodruff*, 260 S.E.2d 775 (N.C. Ct. App. 1979).

61. *J.L.P. v. D.J.P.*, 643 S.W.2d 865 (Mo. Ct. App. 1982); *In re Jane B.*, 380 N.Y.S.2d 848 (Sup. Ct. 1976).

62. *Irish v. Irish*, 300 N.W.2d 739 (Mich. Ct. App. 1980); *Woodruff v. Woodruff*, 260 S.E.2d 775 (N.C. Ct. App. 1979).

63. *J.L.P.*, *supra* note 61.

64. *In re Temos*, 8 Fam. L. Rep. (BNA) 2699 (Pa. Super. Ct. Sept. 10, 1982).

65. *Palmore v. Sidoti*, Fla. App. Dec. 8, 1982 (unreported), *cert. granted*, 104 S. Ct. 271 (1983).

66. *Palmore v. Sidoti*, 104 S. Ct. 1879, 1882 (1974).

67. *In re James M.*, 135 Cal. Rptr. 222 (Ct. App. 1976).

68. *Williams v. Williams*, 432 N.E.2d 375 (Ill. App. Ct. 1982).

69. ALASKA STAT. §25.20.060; CAL. CIV. CODE §4600; COLO. REV. STAT. §14–10–123.5; CONN. GEN. STAT. §46b–56; DEL. CODE ANN. tit. 13, §701; FLA. STAT. §61.13(2)(b); HAWAII REV. STAT. §571–46.1; IDAHO CODE §32–717B; ILL. ANN. STAT. ch. 40, §603.1; IOWA CODE ANN. §598.1; KAN. STAT. ANN §60–1610; KY. REV. STAT. §403–270(3); LA. CIV. CODE ANN. art. 146, 157, 250; ME. REV. STAT. ANN. tit. 19, §§214, 581, 752; MASS. ANN. LAWS ch. 208, §31; MICH. COMP. LAWS ANN. §§722:23(3), 722:23(6a); MINN. STAT. ANN. §§518:0003, 518:17;

Miss. Code Ann. §93–5–23; Mont. Rev. Code Ann. §§40–4–222 to 225; Nev. Rev. Stat. §125.140; N.H. Rev. Stat. Ann. §458.17; N.M. Stat. Ann. §40.4–9.1; N.C. Gen. Stat. §50-13.2(b); Ohio Rev. Code Ann. §3109.04; Or. Rev. Stat. §107.105(1)(b); Pa. Stat. Ann. tit. 23, §§1001–1005, 1011; Tex. Fam. Code §14.06(a); Wis. Stat. Ann. §767.24(1)(b).

70. *Weidner v. Weidner,* 9 Fam. L. Rep. (BNA) 2738 (Iowa Sept. 21, 1983) (not awarded but the court holds that the statute permits it even when one parent objects); *Church v. Church,* 8 Fam. L. Rep. (BNA) 2252 (Mich. Cir. Ct. Dec. 11, 1981) (not requested); *Beck v. Beck,* 432 A.2d 63 (N.J. 1981) (not requested); *In re Wesley, J.K.,* 445 A.2d 1243 (Pa. Super. Ct. 1982) (not requested).

71. For a critical reappraisal of the concept of joint custody, *see* Schulman and Pitt, "Second Thoughts on Joint Child Custody: Analysis of Legislation and Its Implications for Women and Children," 12 *Golden Gate U. L. Rev.* 538 (1982).

APPENDIX

State Statutes Governing Employment, Housing, and Public Accommodations

State	Employment	Housing	Public Accommodations
Ala.	Alaska Stat. §18.80.220	Alaska Stat. §18.80.240	Alaska Stat. §18.80.230
Calif.	Cal. Govt. Code §12940	Cal. Govt. Code §12955	Cal. Civ. Code §51
Colo.	. . . . .	Colo. Rev. Stat. §24-34-502	Colo. Rev. Stat. §24-34-601
Conn.	Conn. Gen. Stat. §46a-60	Conn. Gen. Stat. §46a-63/4	Conn. Gen. Stat. §46a-64
Del.	. . . . .	Del. Code tit. 6 §4603	Del. Code tit. 6 §4504
D.C.	D.C. Code §1-2512	D.C. Code §1-2515	D.C. Code §1-2519
Fla.	Fla. Stat. Ann. §23.167	. . . . .	. . . . .
Hawaii	Haw. Rev. Stat. §378-2	. . . . .	. . . . .
Ill.	Ill. Ann. Stat. ch. 68 §2-102	Ill. Ann. Stat. ch. 68 §1-102	Ill. Ann. Stat. ch. 68 §5-102
Md.	Md. Ann. Code art. 49B §16	Md. Ann. Code art. 49B §20	Md. Ann. Code art. 49B §5

State	Col 1	Col 2	Col 3
Mass.	. . . . . .	Mass. Gen. Laws Ann. ch. 151B §4	. . . . . .
Mich.	Mich. Comp. Laws Ann. §37.2202	Mich. Comp. Laws Ann. §37.2502	Mich. Comp. Laws Ann. §37.2302
Minn.	Minn. Stat. Ann. §363.03(1)	Minn. Stat. Ann. §363.03(2)	. . . . . .
Mont.	Mont. Rev. Codes Ann. §49–2–303	Mont. Rev. Codes Ann. §49–2–305	Mont. Rev. Codes Ann. §49–2–304
N.H.	N.H. Rev. Stat. Ann. §354A:8(1)	N.H. Rev. Stat. Ann. §354A:8(5)	N.H. Rev. Stat. Ann. §354A:8(4)
N.J.	N.J. Stat. Ann. §10:5–12(a)	N.J. Stat. Ann. §10:5–12(g)	N.J. Stat. Ann. §10:5–12(f)
N.Y.	N.Y. Exec. Law §296(1)	N.Y. Exec. Law §296(5)	N.Y. Exec. Law §296(2)
Oreg.	Or. Rev. Stat. §659.030	Or. Rev. Stat. §659.033	Or. Rev. Stat. §659.045
R.I.	. . . . . .	R.I. Gen. Laws §34–37–4	. . . . . .
Wash.	Wash. Rev. Code Ann. §49.60.180	Wash. Rev. Code Ann. §49.60.222	. . . . . .
Wis.	Wis. Stat. Ann. §111.321	Wis. Stat. Ann. §101.22	. . . . . .

AMERICAN CIVIL LIBERTIES UNION HANDBOOKS

SPECIAL MONEY SAVING OFFER

Now you can have an up-to-date listing of Bantam's hundreds of titles plus take advantage of our unique and exciting bonus book offer. A special offer which gives you the opportunity to purchase a Bantam book for only 50¢. Here's how!

By ordering any five books at the regular price per order, you can also choose any other single book listed (up to a $4.95 value) for just 50¢. Some restrictions do apply, but for further details why not send for Bantam's listing of titles today!

Just send us your name and address plus 50¢ to defray the postage and handling costs.

We Deliver!
And So Do These Bestsellers.